SURVIVING THE MEDIA JUNGLE

SURVIVING THE MEDIA JUNGLE

A Practical Guide to Good Media Relations

DINA ROSS

Copyright © 1990 Dina Ross

All rights reserved. No part of this publication may be reproduced, stored in a retrieval system, or transmitted in any form or by any means, electronic, mechanical, photocopying, recording, or otherwise without the prior permission of the publishers.

First published in 1990
by the Mercury Books Division of
W.H. Allen & Co. Plc
Sekforde House, 175/9 St. John Street, London EC1V 4LL

Set in Palatino by
Phoenix Photosetting, Chatham, Kent
Printed and bound in Great Britain by
Biddles Ltd, Guildford and King's Lynn

This book is sold subject to the condition that it shall not, by way of trade or otherwise, be lent, re-sold, hired out or otherwise circulated without the publisher's prior consent in any form of binding or cover other than that in which it is published and without a similar condition including this condition being imposed upon the subsequent purchaser.

British Library Cataloguing in Publication Data
Ross, Dina
 Surviving the media jungle.
 1. Business firms. Public relations
 I. Title
 659.2

 ISBN 1-85251-043-9

FOR MY MOTHER

Contents

Acknowledgements	ix
Introduction: the media jungle	1
1 Defining the terms	9
2 A day in the life of . . .	27
3 Enter Grub Street	43
4 Fishing for angles	59
5 How to write a press release	81
6 Watch the birdie	101
7 Bring on the gin and tonic	115
8 Over the airwaves	145
9 Beyond the press release	177
10 Whingeing and whining	189
11 Some sort of an ending	197
Appendix I Getting started	201
Bibliography	207
Index	209

Acknowledgements

As always in books of this nature, the list of people who have helped and advised, recommended reading material and suggested topics or inclusion is too long to cover fully. However, I would particularly like to thank Professor Norman Hart of Interact Seminars, who suggested my lectures should be compiled in book form and who acted as a generous touchstone for my inquiries; Barbara Levy for her professional guidance; Gerald Rudge, Executive Features Editor of the *Daily Mail*, whose enthusiasm for the project remained undiminished despite my frequent telephone calls; Phil Harding, Editor, the *Today* programme, BBC Radio 4 and Mervyn Hall, News Editor of ITN, for their assistance; *PR Week* for its invaluable Spike or Splash column; and Christie's, the PRCA, IPR, SKY Television and British Satellite Broadcasting for much useful background information.

Grateful thanks to Paul Gillions and Martin Langford at Burson-Marsteller for permission to reproduce their conference checklist and interviewer types; to Michael Bland for sending me his well-constructed booklet 'PR Opportunities in the National Press'; to the *Orpington News Shopper*, British Telecom and the Natural History Museum for permission to reproduce their PR photo-

Surviving the Media Jungle

graphs; to PR Newslink for permission to reproduce a page of its directory; and to *Reader's Digest* for its conference 'grabber'.

Finally a special thank you to my husband for surviving the media jungle with me.

December 1989

Introduction: the media jungle

If public relations can be defined as the art of making a company's products or services desirable, its objectives acceptable and understood by the many audiences it is trying to reach, then media relations is the art of persuading the press that the same organisation is worth talking about.

This is easier said than done. Most journalists find such messages a waste of time, because few organisations bother to find out what journalists really need. The sense of company importance can be so strong that many businessmen cannot accept that what is big news to them is simply a short para on page 6 to a busy sub-editor in a hurry. Businessmen should do their homework. Media relations is a two-way process. That means a very special kind of back-scratching: I'll give your company a mention if you give me the story I'm looking for.

If company personnel – whether public relations officers or not – respect and understand the needs of the media, then it follows quite naturally that the media will be on their side. Nothing succeeds in print or broadcast terms better than a good story, sent to the right person at the right time. It seems, however, that the message still hasn't got through: journalists are still binning useless

Surviving the Media Jungle

press releases that should never have been written, or fobbing off phone calls from earnest PROs that should never have been made.

Good media relations is nothing more than inspired common sense, but there are some basic ground rules and guidelines that need to be followed. And these guidelines have never been more important than in the current growth of the print and broadcast industries.

Marshall McLuhan was right. The medium *is* the message, and as new title follows new title, it's a more telling message than ever before. In the United Kingdom there are some 12,000 media outlets – including national and local papers, consumer and trade magazines, as well as broadcast radio and television.

But the 1980s brought with them a new meaning to the traditional three-pronged targets of newspapers, television and magazines. We have seen the dominance of electronic publishing over age-old printing techniques. Eddie Shah's *Today* newspaper – that brave venture into 24-hour full-colour news – pointed to the way forward. Suddenly, after years of mono-tint newspapers, four TV channels and a selection of trade and consumer publications, it seems as if much of the media world has been turned on its head.

First, there have been the new newspapers, such as the *Independent, Today* and the *Sunday Correspondent*. The rush to hit the headlines has caused inevitable casualties. Some titles have folded, the *Sunday Post* being the most notorious example. The ones that remain have carved out a niche for themselves in the market.

But it's not just newspapers. Over the next ten years the UK broadcasting establishment will be shaken to its very roots. There will be six radio and television chan-

INTRODUCTION: THE MEDIA JUNGLE

nels. A score of new television programmes are already beamed by cable and satellite into the average living room, bringing the consumer more choice. Whether this plethora of programming is filling a worthwhile gap in the market, and is tasteful or edifying, is not within the scope of this book. The fact is it's happening, and happening fast.

How does the businessman cope with this jungle of new media? How can he keep abreast with changes, and harness them to his own corporate objectives? Perhaps even more importantly – does the new media need to be treated any differently from the tried and true avenues of daily newspapers and existing broadcast television?

The aim of this book is to explain how the media – both print and broadcast – work. What are newspapers looking for in terms of stories? How do you reach local television programmes at the right time and in the right way? How do you get the press on your side?

As recently as 10 years ago it was quite common for many British businessmen to look at their company's corporate stance towards the media and say: 'We can afford to ignore the press. We can do very well without press coverage'. But the cut and thrust of 1990s' business life has made that kind of philosophy redundant. An increasingly competitive market place means that businesses must broadcast their 'unique selling proposition' to as wide an audience as possible in order to survive; and the media – print, trade and broadcast – form one of the most crucial channels of communication around. For it is primarily through the media that business reaches its key customer: the consumer.

Today no business can afford to overlook the importance of good press relations. And this applies to anyone in the voluntary sector too – charities or non-profit organisations, for instance, which depend on the media to keep their work in the public eye. Now that deregulation means that charities can advertise on television, the value of third-party endorsement – a mention on a radio programme, a review in a national broadsheet – is essential to consumer acceptance, especially for smaller organisations, which cannot afford the high price of advertisement campaigns.

Let's face it! What would the average man in the street rather believe, an advertisement in a prime slot on commercial television, which he knows has been paid for, or an objective assessment by a reputable journalist on a popular TV programme?

As a nation we read fewer books than any other European country, and gather our news mainly from newspapers and television. Our impressions of products, and our assessment of individual company reputations, are gleaned from what we have read about them in the press, and how they have been portrayed on television. No wonder company chairmen are jostling for one-to-one interviews on Channel 4's *Business Programme* or for exclusive profiles in the *Financial Times*.

Consumer and investigative programmes, such as *That's Life* and *Panorama*, have led to trial by television; and in-depth reports in the Sunday papers and in specialist publications such as *Which?* have either crucified or exonerated many companies and products. The business community has had to readjust to the fact that it is increasingly media-led. The media can after all define or redefine company culture. This can be clearly seen during crises, when the spotlight is constantly trained on each company to justify its actions to the general public.

INTRODUCTION: THE MEDIA JUNGLE

The Zeebrugge ferry disaster in 1987 raised many questions regarding passenger safety and shipowners' liability. But after the initial horror had abated, and these pointed issues were raised with the owners, Townsend Thoresen, the overriding impression the public was left with was that senior management was not particularly concerned with levels of safety or with degrees of compensation. In its dealings with the media Townsend Thoresen came across as brusque, unfeeling and uncommunicative.

Contrast this with the Farley baby milk scare. When traces of salmonella were found to be statistically linked to Farley's plant at Kendal, Cumbria, the whole range of baby milks was withdrawn from circulation and the plant shut down. In addition the Farley spokesmen showed such concern, such a readiness to be open with the general public, such frankness with the press, that the crisis soon blew over and Farley's regained its market share within 18 months.

These varying attitudes reflected themselves in the way the media treated the stories, and it is no coincidence that the Farley crisis received more positive coverage than the incident at Zeebrugge. To this day there will be many who decide not to travel with Townsend Thoresen because of the overriding negative impression that persists, but few remember the Farley crisis and sales are as brisk as ever. No company therefore can ignore the power of the press, and no business can treat media relations as a luxury.

No wonder the public relations industry has mushroomed over the past few years. As more and more companies become aware of the importance of image and company identity, they have turned to PR as an effective means of translating media objectives into marketing objectives. In the UK expenditure on PR reached £550 million at year end 1988, with consultancies averaging a growth rate of 35 per cent a year.

With the opening up of the single European market in 1992 such public relations activity will increase further, as businesses will have to establish EEC as well as UK game plans. Such plans must of necessity consider the European media.

You might think that under such circumstances the relationship between the press and the public relations industry would be a mutually fruitful one, but in fact it is dominated by mistrust and misunderstanding. Even though the barriers are gradually breaking down, the majority of journalists, I suspect, would view the average PR practitioner as a ham-fisted amateur who knows nothing about the way the media operates. The PRO would counter this by saying that the press has never been so arrogant or difficult to deal with, and that the age of cheque-book journalism has led to an abysmal fall in standards.

There is truth on both sides, but realistically it's up to the public relations industry to make the first move. Greater media tolerance will only be achieved by greater PR professionalism. That means recognising and meeting the media's needs without puffery or self-indulgence. (What is ironic is that the national newspapers themselves are spending millions of pounds on PR campaigns to raise their corporate profiles, with the quality broadsheets taking the lead, using both in-house PROs and outside consultancies!)

This is where this book comes in. It can be used by public relations practitioners or by executives who feel

INTRODUCTION: THE MEDIA JUNGLE

they would like to improve their company's relations with the media. It is essentially a practical guide, and is based on lectures on media relations that I have given at the Institute of Marketing and the London Business School.

There have been many worthy books on public relations, but little written about media relations alone. I believe it's because the terms 'public' and 'media' relations are often interchanged and used as synonyms one for the other. But the two terms are different, if complementary, and should never be confused. I have actually seen one writer describe the organising of a competition in a consumer magazine as a 'media relations activity'. It isn't: it's PR pure and simple. But the *placement* of an article in a consumer magazine about a client's product is a media relations exercise.

Of course public relations is much more than pure media relations – and gradually the world of business is coming round to this way of thinking. But the fact remains that no public relations strategy would be complete without a programme of media activity. This guide aims to define the parameters of media relations, and tell you how to set about organising a media strategy for your company or organisation, the pitfalls to watch out for, and the ploys to employ. In the process you should discover that media relations offers very special challenges that can also be a lot of fun.

1

Defining the terms

So – you've decided to embark on a media relations programme. You're going to hit the typewriter, bash out the press release and floor the press with your expertise! But before you start, ask yourself one fundamental question. WHY?

Communications are all very well, but what do you want to achieve by this media activity? What's the impression you want to create? Who are you trying to reach? And are you wasting your time?

Even before you contact the press, it's important to define your objectives. It's the same in any marketing strategy, and in media relations terms *the most successful press campaigns are those which translate your company's* marketing and corporate *objectives into media objectives*.

There are many reasons why a media campaign is worth pursuing. Here are just some of them:

- Your company is launching a new product, and you want consumers to know about it.

- Your company is changing its profile: this may be as the result of a takeover, or a radical departure in company philosophy, product range or personnel.

- Your company is rebuilding its image after a crisis.

Surviving the Media Jungle

- Your company's products are well-known and established, but you need to target new users.
- Your company's products or services are misunderstood or misused by the target audience.
- Your company has a bad record in employee communications.
- Your company needs to inform civil servants of its activities or wishes to lobby politicians.
- Your company needs to attract new investors and encourage the loyalty of existing shareholders.

In fact the list is endless, and each company or product creates its own audience and its own media. Assuming you have a genuine reason for launching a media relations campaign, a brainstorming session is a good way of focusing on your company's needs and requirements before you even start.

One useful way of doing this is to take a large sheet of paper and divide it into two halves, one called *Communications objectives*, the second called *Relevant media*.

Communications objectives

Under Communications objectives list all the reasons for the media campaign, the people you want to attract, the messages you wish to give out, and the problems you may face in doing so.

Take the example of Exclusive Cars Ltd. It makes a do-it-yourself car kit, aimed at males aged 25–45. The car is a

DEFINING THE TERMS

replica of a 1948 MG-A. It has all the features of a period sports car – leather seats, retractable canvas top, wooden steering wheel and dashboard – plus the modern advantages of power steering, fridge tucked under the back seat, and cruise control. The kit costs £9,500 and can be assembled in 8–12 weeks.

How is Exclusive going to organise its media campaign?

Start with communications objectives. Exclusive must first define the audience it wants to reach:

1 Who is the company aiming at? (product audience)

- Males aged 25–45.
- Do-it-yourself enthusiasts.
- Fairly affluent individuals who have enough money and time to spend on building the model sports car.

2 What does the company want to tell them? (product messages/benefits)

- The Exclusive kit is a unique opportunity for the DIY car builder to assemble a superb period car.
- The car is easy to assemble, and it looks superb.
- The car has the vintage looks but runs like a new car.
- The car has an excellent safety record, and is economical to run.
- It's the kind of car most people dream of owning but can never afford.

Surviving the Media Jungle

- The kit is cost-effective: for the price of a secondhand Jaguar you can build an original and eye-catching sports car.

3 What do they know about the company? (product status)

Exclusive Cars is a well-established company, with an excellent reputation as vintage car restorers. But car kits are a new departure: Exclusive is venturing into uncharted territory.

4 What are the problems the company will face? (product threats)

- At £9,500 the car kit is priced at premium level. Compared to the cost of buying and restoring a genuine vintage, it is cheap. But set against other car kits it is by far the most expensive.

- Will car kit builders buy the MG-A look-alike from a newcomer to the market place?

This is a basic communications plan, and the next step is to define the relevant media who will help you in your task. Now you will have to do your research, and work out the right plan of action for your company's message. All the benefits and problems of your company's products or services will have to be addressed, and it's important that you get the media mix right, because it's through the press that you will reach the bulk of your target audiences.

Relevant media

Media selection is not a case of sticking a pin in a telephone book and hoping for the best. There are many media directories that can help, and these have been assembled in Appendix I, p. 201.

You can find these directories – *Brad, Willings, Editors, PNA*, for example – in the reference section of your local library, but it's a good investment to have one or two directories on hand in your office. You will use them constantly. The directories list all media, national newspapers, magazines, trade and consumer publications, freesheets, radio and television stations, by name, type and circulation, and include an invaluable list of contact names and phone numbers. Most directories are updated each year, and some, such as PR Newslink's *Editors*, are updated quarterly (see illustration of page from *Editors*).

A caveat, though! However accurate these reference books are, some of their information is bound to be out of date even by the time they go to press. I often think that following a journalist's career path is a bit like a game of musical chairs – it's quite usual to find that the editor of the cookery page of *Woman's Own*, who was your contact only last month, has now left to head up a similar position on *Woman's Realm*. There is only one way round this, and that is to do a regular ring-round, about every 6 months, to check that your contact is still there, or to find out who his replacement is if he's moved on.

What media, then, are you trying to reach? Most companies would probably say 'as many outlets as possible!' In the UK alone there are just over 12,000 different media outlets, including national newspapers and TV stations,

Surviving the Media Jungle

637-150
DAN AIR IN-FLIGHT INTERNATIONAL
JEM Publishing Ltd
20a Eastcheap
Letchworth, Herts.
SG6 3DE

Tel: 0462 679347
Fax: 0462 670214
Freq: 4
C: 1000000
P: JEM Publishing Ltd

Editor – Michael A James

Publication Profile
Published April, July, October and January.

637-202
THE EUROPEAN
Chiltern House
184 High Street
Berkhamsted, Herts
HP4 3AP

Tel: 0442 875431
Fax: 0442 863152
Freq: 4
C: 250000
P: Dennis Fairey & Associates Ltd

Editor – Jack Prosser

Publication Profile
In-flight magazine of Air Europe.

637-210
FLIGHTPATH
Highfield House
2 Highfield Avenue
Newbury, Berks
RG14 5DS

Tel: 0635 38888
Freq: 4
P: Kingsclere Contract Publishing Ltd

Publication Profile
The Inflight Magazine of Gulf Air, General Interest features, travel, art, food.

637-220
HIGH LIFE
Athene House
66–73 Shoe Lane
London
EC4P 4AB

Tel: 01–377 4633
Telex: 922488 BUREAU G
Telex Ref: HWY
Freq: 12
C: 215000
P: Headway Publications Limited

Editor – William Davis

Publication Profile
Distributed through British Airways

637-260
HOT AIR
108 Canalot Studios
222 Kensal Road
London
W10 5BN

Tel: 01–969 7120
Fax: 01–968 7782
Freq: 3
C: 85000
P: John Brown Publishing Limited

Editor – John Brown

Publication Profile
Distributed to passengers on Virgin Atlantic Airways. Joint Editors: Caroline Wheal and John Brown

637–320
MANX TAILS
48 Alexander Drive
Douglas
Isle of Man

Page from *Editors*

DEFINING THE TERMS

as well as local freesheets. How many are reached of course depends on the strength of the story you are trying to sell, and the angles it provides – we'll look at angles in depth in Chapter 4 – but generally the media list should be divided into the following core areas:

National daily and Sunday newspapers.
Local newspapers and freesheets.
National radio and television programmes.
Local radio and television programmes.
Cable and satellite television programmes.
Consumer and trade publications.
Electronic information systems, e.g. Prestel/Teletext.
Press agencies and wire services.
Freelance journalists.
Foreign press: the London correspondents of major international newspapers and broadcasting organisations can also be contacted if your story has a strong international flavour.

How should Exclusive make up its list? This is a test question. Have a go. Now try and make up a list concerning your own company or product.

Once you have chosen the appropriate media outlets, you should make sure they are written down, filed and circulated to any executive likely to deal with the press. This list should also be sent to your press cuttings agency, which will scan newspapers and magazines for you and forward relevant cuttings for your files. You will probably find that if you issue press releases on a fairly regular basis, the same names on the list will crop up time and again. Media lists stored on computer discs are standard practice now and make good sense: names,

Surviving the Media Jungle

addresses and phone numbers can be regularly checked and updated in the most efficient way possible. If you don't have a computer, typed lists and addressographs systems are an effective, if slow-moving, alternative.

You may say that making a list is all very well – but how do you know which media to choose? That all depends on your target audience. Exclusive Cars knows precisely who it is trying to reach: so must you. If you've defined your marketing and PR campaign correctly, the relevant media will follow automatically.

Social grade		Newspapers
A	**Upper middle class**	*The Times, Financial Times, Sunday Times*
B	**Middle class** – right of centre	*Daily Telegraph, The Times, Sunday Times, Sunday Telegraph, Financial Times*
B	**Middle class** – left of centre/ liberal, intellectual	*Guardian, Independent, Independent on Sunday, Observer, Sunday Correspondent*
C1	**Lower middle class** **White-collar workers**	*Daily Express, Daily Mail, Today, Sunday Express, Mail on Sunday*
C2	**Skilled working class** **Blue-collar workers**	*Daily Mirror, Sun, Star, Sunday Mirror, Sunday People, News of the World, Sunday Sport*
D	**Semi-skilled working class**	*Daily Mirror, Sun, Star, Sunday Mirror, Sunday People, News of the World, Sunday Sport*
E	**Unemployed, other groups (e.g. homeless)**	*Daily Mirror, Sun, Star, Sunday Mirror, Sunday People, News of the World, Sunday Sport*

DEFINING THE TERMS

For trade and consumer publications there is no harm phoning up the advertising departments and asking for an audience profile. They will be very happy to send you the relevant documentation – after all, you may be a potential advertiser! When it comes to radio and television programmes on both BBC and independent stations, publicity departments will be able to give you audience breakdowns to help you in your research. You can also find out a lot of programme information by consulting such publications as *TV Times* and *Radio Times*.

National newspapers are easier to pigeonhole. Each has a clearly defined audience. The *Sun* has the highest circulation of any newspaper in the UK – about 4 million – but its readers will probably not be readers of the *Financial Times*. Yet readers of *The Times* or the *Daily Telegraph* (circulation 441,000 and 1.13m respectively) may well take a second newspaper, say the *Daily Mail* (cir. 1.80m), for a little light relief. It's all to do with class structure and aspirations. A rough-and-ready guide to Who Reads What in the UK can be seen on page 16.

Remember that few stories will suit all media in the same way. In fact newspapers will report a story in markedly dissimilar ways. Take this story, variously reported in *The Times*, *Daily Mail* and *Daily Mirror*.

The Times's story on listeria-infected pâté, 14 July 1989

Listeria pâté danger was known two months ago

By Michael Hornsby and Michael Binyon

The Department of Health admitted last night that it learned of the discovery of listeria in pâté two months ago, but decided against a public warning at the time.

'Everything suggested that it was a local problem in a par-

Surviving the Media Jungle

ticular store, probably caused by poor handling. There was no reason to suppose that there might be a problem at the manufacturing stage,' an official said.

The admission is certain to refuel the debate about the Government's alleged slowness in alerting the public to threats to food safety, which began with the salmonella-in-eggs affair last December.

Ms Harriet Harman, Labour spokeswoman on health, last night called for the setting up of an independent food standards agency because it was obvious the Government 'is not prepared to act decisively to protect the health of the consumer'.

Meanwhile, the listeria-in-pâté rumpus turned into an international dispute yesterday when the chairman of the Belgian factory suspected of supplying the infected products insisted that they had been uncontaminated when they left his premises.

'I am 100 per cent certain that the pâté left here in a perfect state. We have never had any complaints before.

'We have regular weekly checks on food safety and we have the highest standards', Mr Paul Peeters, chairman of Sanpareil, a Nestlé subsidiary, told journalists.

Belgian health ministry inspectors last night gave the factory a clean bill of health, but said exports to Britain would be suspended for a week while further tests were carried out. Production for the Belgian market will continue.

'We are surprised that the factory can say so categorically they have not got listeria when their own government has suspended exports,' said a spokesman for Gateway, the supermarket chain in one of whose Welsh stores the listeria was first found on May 11.

Mattessons, the Banbury-based company which imports the Belgian pâté and supplies 20 per cent of the British market, said it had carried out its own tests, using a technique only developed in the last few months, and that these had detected unacceptable levels of listeria in prepacked pâté from the Belgian factory.

The company said that all pâtés imported from Belgium

were pre-packed by the factory. 'I find it very hard to believe how the pâtés could have become contaminated en route from the factory to us,' a spokesman said.

Mr Alan Brown, of the environmental health office at the Rhymney Valley District Council, said the samples taken from the Gateway stores had included both unopened pre-packed pâté and opened pâtés on display at the delicatessen counter. 'We found higher levels of listeria in pâté on display, but that does not prove that handling was necessarily at fault'.

Gateway admitted last night that after the initial finding of listeria two months ago it had taken the Belgian pâté off the shelves of its store in Caerphilly, only to put it back again three days later after consulting local environmental health officers.

Mr Brown disputed Gateway's claim that it had been given permission to return the pâté to the shelves. He said his officers started testing pâtés on May 11 after a Welsh housewife had complained of a stomach upset.

They took six samples of pâté from Gateway's Caerphilly store and found that every one was contaminated. Further tests at a Gateway store in Pontypridd found listeria in two samples. The Public Health Laboratory Service confirmed the presence of listeria and alerted the Department of Health. 'They have known for a considerable length of time,' Mr Brown said.

The Department of Health continued to insist last night that it was only last Tuesday evening, when the results of Mattessons' own tests were given to them, that there was 'the first clear evidence that there might be a problem at point of manufacture'. On Wednesday, the department issued its warning to pregnant woman and other vulnerable groups.

How the poisoned pâté crisis was investigated

The timetable of events surrounding the listeria crisis:
- **May 11:** Rhymney Valley District Council environmental health officers take samples of pâté from Gate-

Surviving the Media Jungle

way store in Caerphilly.
- **May 19:** Public Health Laboratory Service (PHLS) confirms listeria finding.
- **May 22 – June 5:** More samples taken at Gateway stores. Some found to have high listeria levels.
- **June 20–26:** Further samples at Gateway store in Pontypridd.
- **July 3:** PHLS advises Welsh Office and Dept of Health of persistent problem, probably due to handling.
- **July 6:** Suppliers warned of possible problem at Belgian factory.
- **July 11:** Suppliers say tests indicate problem at factory.
- **July 12:** Government issues public health warning.

Daily Mail's story on listeria-infected pâté, 14 July 1989

'Poison' pâté found months before public was warned

Report by CHRISTOPHER WARD

INFECTED samples of Belgian pâté were discovered two months before Government officials issued their public health warning, it emerged yesterday.

Environmental health officers in Wales say they found the deadly listeria bug in samples of meat spread as long ago as mid-May.

Until yesterday's disclosure it was believed the Government's warning to pregnant women and other people at risk had been delayed for just five days.

As the fresh evidence emerged last night, MPs renewed their attack on the Government for failing to act more swifly.

Samples

The Belgian health ministry also banned the export of

three types of pâté made at the factory at the centre of the row.

In Britain, the timetable leading to the Government health warning was disclosed by officials of Rhymney Valley council in Mid-Glamorgan. This is it:

On May 11, environmental health inspectors take samples of pâté from a Gateway supermarket in Caerphilly.

May 19: Tests prove they are infected and stocks are immediately withdrawn by the store.

May 22: Stocks are back on the shelves at the same store. Further samples are taken from there and two other supermarkets. Two samples contain listeria – both from Gateway in Caerphilly.

May 25: Eight samples are taken from the same store. Seven prove positive. Samples taken subsequently in other areas of South Wales, including Cardiff and Pontypridd, also prove positive.

June 16: The public health laboratories contact the Department of Health, informing them of the findings.

July 12: The Government issues a public warning.

Alan Brown, principal environmental health officer for Rhymney Valley said finding the listeria bug was 'pure luck'.

'We received a complaint from a house-wife who contracted gastro-enteritis and decided to do a routine check,' he said. 'The listeria test was an afterthought.'

Mr Roy Hughes, Labour MP for Newport, described the delay as 'alarming' and demanded an inquiry.

But a Health Department spokesman said: 'As soon as we discovered the contamination originated at the factory we issued a public warning.'

Belgium's health ministry yesterday banned the export of turkey, duck and Brussels pâté made at the Sanpareil factory near Antwerp, pending the results of more tests. Sanpareil claimed that its pâté was safe when it left the factory.

Surviving the Media Jungle

Daily Mirror's story on listeria-infected pâté, 14 July 1989

HEALTH CHIEFS' 2-MONTH SILENCE ON PÂTÉ

By IAN CAMERON, GORDON HAY and SYDNEY YOUNG

THE deadly listeria food bug was found in imported Belgian pâté almost TWO MONTHS AGO.

But, despite repeated warnings, Government health chiefs did nothing to alert the public until Wednesday this week.

Last night a major row erupted over who should carry the can for the astonishing gaffe.

The bug was first found on May 19 in samples taken from a Gateway supermarket at Caerphilly, South Wales.

The store cleared suspect tubs of pâté from its shelves – but, three days later, they were put back on sale.

Local Rhymney Valley health officials insist that the decision was taken by Gateway's own experts.

Gateway claim they were told that the laboratory tests were inconclusive and the pâté could go back on sale.

The area's environmental health officer Alan Brown said yesterday: 'In our opinion it shouldn't have been returned to the shelves – even the slightest risk to health cannot be taken.'

Tested

Later samples also showed listeria infection, said Mr Brown.

He said the Department of Health was aware of the listeria problem in mid-June – four weeks before they issued Wednesday's warning.

The Department was alerted by Public Health Service officials at Cardiff's University Hospital who had tested the contaminated pâté. But a spokesman for the Department in London said: 'We felt it was a local handling problem in a shop in South Wales.

'It wasn't until earlier this week that it was felt it was a potential national problem

DEFINING THE TERMS

> and the warnings were issued.'
>
> Gateway bosses say they acted swiftly once they obtained a copy of the latest analysis from the Department of Health.
>
> Spokeswoman Debbie Young said: 'As soon as we knew there was a potentially serious problem we removed the pâté from our shelves.'
>
> The Government now faces a Commons probe over its silence on the danger.

What this exercise shows is that news is interpreted differently by different publications. It's a difference in style, political standpoint as well as readership. The same differences can be seen in radio and television programmes. BBC 1's *The Money Programme*, for instance, which is aimed at the average saver and investor with a small portfolio, is much less sophisticated than Channel 4's *Business Programme*, which is watched by industry leaders, chairmen and executives of multi-national companies.

There are differences in style and tone in radio too. The news bulletins of such commercial stations as LBC or Red Rose Radio are more whacky and popular in tone and content than the national BBC bulletins, which, true to their 'public service broadcasting' image, still favour a more sedate approach.

Different media need to be approached in different ways, because their requirements are different and specialised. One way to do this is to 'tailor-make' your press releases to suit (see Chapter 5, p. 81).

The only way to understand the media is to read, view and listen widely. Get a feel for the style of different newspapers and trade magazines, and the kind of stories they look for; hear how radio approaches news and

Surviving the Media Jungle

features; look at television programmes critically, noting the differences between BBC and Independent stations, the tone of current affairs and feature programmes. This will also enable you to identify news opportunities to follow up.

If you do this, you will soon discover one of the fundamental truths about the media: that there is a mystique surrounding the industry which should not in fact exist at all. The smell of printer's ink, the pressure of the deadline, the hot-shot cub reporter relentlessly pursuing his story, are myths fostered by Hollywood. Lois Lane and Citizen Kane have a lot to answer for. Similarly sensational novels, such as Julie Burchill's *Ambition*, portray Fleet Street hacks as sex- and power-hungry megalomaniacs with superhuman appetites.

The truth is less romantic: newspapers, television and radio programmers are in the business of making money. They know what consumers want, and they provide it in the form the consumers expect: a tabloid story in the *Sun* will of course be reported differently in a broadsheet like *The Times*, if it makes *The Times* at all.

Which is not to say that the media is not in the business of providing entertainment. It's why top journalists, such as Jean Rook, Sir Robin Day and Brian Redhead, are always in work: they not only report the news, they reflect it with their particular and idiosyncratic styles. In their own way they are entertainers, and the news, by definition, becomes a part of show business.

It's why such shock-scandal stories as the Profumo affair and the Guinness insider-dealing trials make front-page headlines. Of course it's news, but the reaction it provokes in the consumer is not unlike the sit-bolt-upright-and-gasp effect of a horror film: the reading and

DEFINING THE TERMS

viewing publics may shake their heads and tut-tut, but they are secretly titillated by being offended.

It's also why sob-cruelty-to-child-or-animal stories are also prevalent, especially in the popular press. Nothing attracts readers, listeners or viewers more than a real tearjerker. Writers of romantic fiction, war movies and sentimental musicals have known this for years. Just reflect a moment. When was the last time you saw good news making a front-page headline? Gloom and doom does it all the time. The industry adage 'Bad news makes good news' may be a cliché, but you can always spot the 'journo' – he's the one who is running to the scene of the disaster, rather than away from it!

Pedlars of press releases and company 'exclusives' should bear this in mind when they try to sell their wares. I'm not suggesting they should deliberately seek out the skeletons in the cupboard, or immediately adopt a Kampuchean refugee, but they should always be aware of the USP (the unique selling proposition) that would make a journalist's eyes gleam.

Most company press stories are not news-based, they are feature-based – and the difference is important. News is here and now, immediate, of national and international concern. It is finite: nothing is more useless to a journalist than yesterday's story. But feature material has the potential to be evergreen. It will not kill the *Independent*'s front page or *News At Ten*'s ratings if the latest low-calorie soft drink to come on the market is not reported. But no one will forgive them if they miss the appearance of a cure for AIDS.

Feature material has to have something that is a notch above the rest in order to be used. That 'something' can be explained in many ways: there has to be a good story

Surviving the Media Jungle

or angle, certainly, but it's a story that has to be attractively packaged, well-presented and researched. If the approach is via a press release, that communiqué must be written in a way that is accessible to and instantly understood by the journalist it is trying to reach.

How is that done? Let's go back one step, and first look at the way print, radio and broadcast journalists work. Though the three media are very different, they're united in one common pursuit: the hunt for news.

2

A day in the life of . . .

The *Daily Mail* features desk

It's 6.30 am on a Wednesday morning. Gerald Rudge, executive features editor of the *Daily Mail*, switches on Radio 4. The *Today* programme is mandatory listening for any newspaper man: it not only gives succinct updates on what's in the news, but somewhere within its format may be hidden the 'golden nuggets' – the germs of what may possibly become features in the next day's *Mail*.

The headlines indicate it's a low news day. There's the usual depressing collection of foreign items – South Africa, the Middle East, Northern Ireland – but no heart-searing tragedies. From a features point of view that's good news. Plenty of opportunities to flesh out the paper with the kind of human interest 'people' stories so characteristic of the paper's style.

Over coffee Gerald Rudge reads the *Mail* and the *Express*, with one ear still cocked to *Today*, and makes notes. There's one particular story that's caught his fancy: a new corkscrew has just come on to the market, retailing at £39.99. For that kind of money the discerning imbiber ought to get something pretty special, and this corkscrew is computerised, powered by a silicone chip

Surviving the Media Jungle

which not only prints out the vintage of the wine, and at what temperature it should be served, but also, would you believe, whether the peasants washed their feet before trampling the grapes!

Rudge checks the calendar. No, it isn't 1 April. How could you run the story? Why not get a reporter to check the corkscrew out with three wine experts, such as Jancis Robinson, Oz Clarke and the Savoy's maître d'hôtel?

He drives to the office, still listening to Radio 4. The 'Best of British Youth Awards' competition has just been announced. The winners will be revealed in 6 weeks' time. He files the information away for future use.

By 8.30 am he's at his desk. He carefully reads all the other national dailies, and there's even time for a quick flick through the post. The average daily intake of 250-odd press releases from PR companies has arrived. They're usually divided up between his team, but he can't resist a preview: after all, even though 80 per cent of them are dross and pure client 'puffs', you never know . . .

By 10.00 am, most of the *Mail*'s journalists are at their word processors. It's not that journalists are lazy and sleep in late, it's just that many reporters prefer to read the daily papers in the comfort of their own homes. There's the usual good-natured banter about the latest sex scandal in the House of Commons before they settle down to business.

At 10.30 am comes the features editorial general conference. Rudge's meeting is attended by the deputy features editor, the assistant features editor, the editor of Femail (the women's section), and the features assistant. Ideas for tomorrow's features are kicked around: the lead feature concerns the image of the Royal Family, following confirmation that the Princess Royal's marriage is on the rocks; there's also a feature on a well-known TV actress's battle against cancer; and two press releases could inspire 'shorts' – the paragraphs sandwiched at the bottom of the main feature pages which make interesting snippets of news and 'break up' the main feature columns.

To get the balance right they are still looking for something light and amusing. Rudge mentions the intelligent corkscrew, and the deputy features editor suggests they try one out at El Vino's – editorial conferences are genial affairs. By the end of the meeting about twelve possible features have been identified, including the main picture 'spread' for the centre pages. Everyone knows that those twelve ideas will probably be whittled down to three or four by the end of the day. Rudge then discusses his plans with the *Mail*'s editor or, in his absence, the deputy editor.

Time to hit the phone to commission outside writers. *Daily Mail* feature writers are given their respective assignments, interviews are lined up. Sometime after 11 am Gerald Rudge attends the main news conference in the editor's office.

The news conference is chaired by the editor, and attended by the deputy and assistant editors, the news editor, the foreign news editor, the picture editor, the show-business editor and the sports editor, all of whom have already held their respective departmental meetings, and Rudge in this instance is very much an impartial observer.

The conference begins with a brief post-mortem on the previous day's paper, and then gets down to its main purpose: charting the course for the following day's

Surviving the Media Jungle

news. Each editor reads out his story list or 'schedule', and the way individual stories should be developed and angled is discussed and agreed.

But immediately after the conference there's a sudden change of plan. A PR contact has telephoned Rudge to tell him that he has learnt that one of the opposition papers has found out about the exclusive interview the *Mail* has had with the Duchess of York, and is intending to write a 'spoiler' – an article written from press cuttings, but cleverly disguised to make it look like contemporary material. This obviously calls for a swift change of editorial tactics.

Rudge immediately informs his deputy, and they plan the counter-attack: the actress' fight for life will run, but it will now have to be pushed back from the centre pages to make room for Fergie's interview, which had been planned for later in the week, but which must now be brought forward. It looks like a good, strong edition. Time for lunch.

2.30 pm: Gerald Rudge looks on afternoons at the features desk as a steady build-up to the climax of the day.

By 4.00 pm the first of the planned features has been written by staff, and outside contributors phone through, telex or fax their copy in by 5.00 pm. The features executives and sub-editors are in their element now – combing through and rewriting untidy copy, tightening, thinking up lively headlines, pasting up. Pictures are also coming in, including some wonderful photos of Fergie at home.

Rudge and an assistant editor read all features copy, and then, with the editor, finally decide on the main leader page feature article. Obviously tomorrow it will be the Duchess of York, but features are never predictable – other leads are often decided late in the day. It is only at the 6.00 pm evening conference that the 'splash' – the front page lead – and other news pages are decided.

New technology has transformed the *Mail*, as it has every other daily newspaper. The subs create the paper on their computer screens, and old-style printing blocks, which used to take at least 30 minutes to produce, can now be formulated in half the time. There's greater flexibility of type sizes, very soon the advantage of easily produced full-colour pictures, and deadlines for important feature stories for the first edition have been put back to 8. 00 pm. For conventional feature material and PR-based stories, though, the deadline of 4.30 pm still applies.

By 8.00 pm it's an 'early' night; a page proof of the main leader page is read and approved. Meanwhile Rudge is already thinking about Friday's edition. He has noted that the water privatisation debate is hotting up – there's definitely room for a 'think piece' by a controversial MP. He asks his deputy to commission it. One of his writers reports that the intelligent corkscrew has been given the thumbs down by the pundits, but the photographer has taken some great pictures. It goes down on Gerald Rudge's list as a good possible piece on page 10.

The *Today* programme, BBC Radio 4

When news of the Hillsborough football tragedy broke out, Philip Harding, editor of the *Today* programme, was

Surviving the Media Jungle

at home, enjoying a quiet weekend with his family. Then news came over the radio that ninety-five football fans had been crushed to death in a sudden uncontrollable crowd-surge at Sheffield Wednesday's ground, which was hosting the FA Cup semi-final.

It was 5.10 pm on Saturday 15 April 1989. Clearly this was a major crisis, and a major story. It had to be handled with the greatest tact, and also the greatest speed. How would *Today*, the most popular news programme in the UK, listened to by 6 million people, cover the tragedy?

Phil Harding phoned his deputy, and they discussed the possibilities. There could be a special news programme about the disaster the following day – but they felt that to replace the religious programme *Sunday* after such events might be viewed as insensitive; alternatively Monday morning's *Today* could devote several in-depth reports to the disaster.

After consultation with senior BBC management, they opted for the second course. Editorially as well as emotionally the story was centred on Liverpool rather than Sheffield, for it was Liverpool's fans who had suffered. Phone calls were made: a team of two producers, two reporters and a senior editor were despatched to Liverpool – they were to work out of the BBC's local radio base, Radio Merseyside, relaying their stories by direct link to the *Today* studios.

Locating Brian Redhead, who would present the programme from Liverpool, was more of a problem. He was on holiday in the Lake District, and was eventually contacted late on Saturday night. Cutting his holiday short, he too was en route to Liverpool early Sunday morning.

Cool heads are essential for reporting on crises, and there is no room for panic. Editorial judgements must be

A DAY IN THE LIFE OF . . .

sharp, focused and all-embracing. Every facet of the tragedy had to be covered, from the grief-stricken relatives left behind to the problem of safety in football grounds in general. At the same time world and UK news headlines should not be neglected: there had to be a balance between reporting on the specifics and the generalities.

The format of Monday's programme was worked out early Sunday morning by Phil Harding and his team, and refined throughout the day, as more news filtered through. Final editorial decisions were taken at 8.00 pm on Sunday evening.

At 7.00 am there was a report by Brian Redhead live outside Liverpool's Roman Catholic Cathedral, as mass was in progress. The report only lasted 4 minutes, but remains, to my mind, one of the most poignant and moving pieces of journalism in the language. It made *Pick of the Week*, and deservedly so, showing as it did the human face of Liverpool in mourning.

Hillsborough was of course the exception to the rule. Most days are hectic in current affairs news programmes, but less emotionally draining. *Today* prides itself on being first with any story – 'You heard it first on Today' is as much a motto as a slogan – and it requires a team with a special ability at 'double-think' to predict the following morning's headlines, keeping the programme as topical and up-to-the-minute as possible.

Today runs for two and a half hours – from 6.30 am to 9. 00 am – Monday to Saturday. There are between twenty-two and twenty-six separate stories and features broadcast daily, which is a lot of news coverage.

Programme ideas come from two main sources – editorial conference and forward planning. Both TV and

Surviving the Media Jungle

radio stations have forward planning editors, to whom news of forthcoming events should be sent. They issue a weekly diary of noteworthy news/arts/and PR events, covering the current month, to all editorial staff.

Today's forward planning editor has a team of two producers and researchers, and they will be working with reporters to put together material – 'evergreen' fillers and soon-to-be topical stories – for the programme. This ensures *Today* has a constant supply of varied stories and features to flesh out the diet of news.

Forward planning editors always attend the 10.15 am news conference. It is chaired by the day editor and includes the whole programme team.

By this time all editorial staff have read the morning papers, and probably caught the headlines on a television programme such as BBC's *Breakfast Time*. Ideas for both tomorrow's programme and forward planning features are discussed, and an initial menu listed. About 50 per cent of the menu will be kept; the rest will change as the emphasis on the day's news changes, and as events unfold throughout the day.

Producers and reporters are given their assignments – some will be putting together stories for tomorrow's *Today*, and others will be working on forward planning ideas for two or three days hence. The day's schedule of interviewing, scripting links, making travel arrangements, and booking guests into studio, begins.

During the day Phil Harding and his day editor will be keeping abreast of the developments in the news, and liaising with reporters on progress. It is also one of the times the daily batch of press releases – usually about 5 feet's worth of paper – is combed through. Most releases are immediately discarded. Harding has little time for PR approaches, finding them badly targeted and normally of scant use to the programme.

I was shown a release from a major manufacturer of tea, announcing the appointment of a new marketing director; another from a computer company relocating to new premises in Warrington. Neither was of interest to the programme. The computer company should have contacted its local radio station if it wanted coverage. The tea manufacturer had missed the point of the programme completely: *Today* is a hard news programme, it doesn't deal in company appointments unless they coincide with a major industrial or financial story of national concern.

Harding is a newsman down to his boots – frippery annoys him, unprofessionalism angers him, but what irritates him most is that PROs don't seem to listen to *Today* and understand its needs. He is constantly being bombarded by phone calls from persistent public relations executives who insist that he attends some totally useless press conference. He is unapologetically brusque, to put it mildly, in his replies.

By late afternoon reporters are gradually coming back to Broadcasting House. They will edit their taped interviews and write their scripts. Some, who have had several interviews to conduct or who have had far to travel, will come back late that evening, editing and recording late into the night. Most stories are completed, however, by about 10.30 pm.

The news team listens to Radio 4's five o'clock news programme, *PM*, and watches the BBC six o'clock news on television. The first fine-tuning is made. If an urgent story breaks, reporters will be despatched to the scene. The team is now ready to hand over, at about 8.00 pm, to

Surviving the Media Jungle

the night editor and his team – two producers and one reporter.

Throughout the day and into the night live interviews are set up for the programme. There is a policy that no one is contacted after 12.00 midnight or before 6.30 am – although in a crisis such courtesies are necessarily abandoned. The night team will watch the BBC nine o'clock news on television, and probably ITN's *News at Ten*. If *Today* finds that TV is covering a non-headline story that it was going to schedule, it drops the story instantly: the slogan 'you heard it first on Today' must remain true.

During the night journalists are constantly scanning the pages of the following day's papers looking for news. More than thirty copies of all national newspapers are delivered to the newsrooms by 10.30 pm, so that the team can be first in.

The presenters arrive at the *Today* studios at 4.30 am. They have 2 hours in which to catch up on the news, read the papers, assimilate the running order of the programme, take briefings for the live interviews they will be conducting and write their scripts. Then, at 6.30 am precisely, it's on air once again.

This is high-pressure work for journalists at the most talented end of the spectrum. It needs to be, because *Today* is the programme that counts most of our captains of industry and politicians – including the prime minister – among its regular daily audience. It remains the UK's most successful news programme on radio precisely because it sets itself high standards and almost impossible deadlines. But, as Phil Harding would say, that's all in a day's work.

A DAY IN THE LIFE OF . . .

News at Ten

There's a scene in the film *Broadcast News* where, with only seconds to spare before going on air, an urgent news videotape is rushed to the transmission room. In her rush to get to the unit the poor secretary in charge of the tape trips over a trolley, hurtles into unsuspecting passers-by and suffers numerous bruises. But the tapes gets there on time. Panic is averted, and the secretary brushes herself down to deal with another crisis or three.

According to Mervyn Hall, ITN's news editor, such dramas are not unusual in television, and add to the spice of life. In fact there does seem to be an air of organised chaos throughout the newsroom. Everyone talks loudly, moves quickly. There are programmes to get out. Today. No point hanging about – right?

Of course right. Mervyn Hall himself has been in the office since 6.30 am. He's already listened to the bulletins on the World Service and the News Briefing at 6.00 am on Radio 4, and tuned into LBC, London's Independent Radio News station, while driving to work.

Over cups of coffee he'll be looking at the newspaper headlines, and catching the breakfast programmes on the two TV monitors in his office. The morning diet is a mixture of BBC's *Breakfast Time*, *TV-am*, Channel 4's morning show and *SKY News*, the satellite channel.

It sounds exhausting, but television news people develop an uncanny habit of being able to do several things at once. Perhaps it's the fact that television mixes pictures and sound, with a liberal helping of graphics as well. There's a definite need for versatility.

News of course doesn't keep office hours. When the

Surviving the Media Jungle

day news team arrives about 8.00 am, one of the first things its members will do is to check with the night news team to see how stories have developed overnight. The night news team – home and foreign editors, producer, two scriptwriters, reporter and newsreader – have been responsible for the night bulletins at 1.00 am, 2.00 am and 5.00 am. They have produced a menu of current events which will probably form the backbone of that night's *News at Ten*.

The current events menu is discussed at the first morning editorial meeting, which takes place at 8.10 am. The night news editor will give a brief summary of the main points of the news so far, and the day news team will take over from there. It's a standard editorial conference, attended by home, sports and foreign editors, producers, and the programme editors of ITN's three main bulletins: *News at One*, *News at 5.40 pm* and *News at Ten*. The editors of the 'shorts' – the five-minute TV news summaries which go out at 9.55 am, 10.55 am and 11.55 am – will also be present.

Each programme editor will assign reporters and scriptwriters to individual news items, and brief them on the nature of the story. They know full well that several stories will be dropped from the agenda as the day progresses. The 8.10 am meeting is very much a preliminary editorial conference, but it provides the skeleton for the final product.

It's also time to talk to Assignments, which is the office responsible for the allocation of camera crews and mobile edit units for tight-deadline stories. Crews are always in short supply, and finding the right number of cameramen and technicians to cover every story is a delicate juggling act. Hard news must of course be a priority

A DAY IN THE LIFE OF . . .

– something Mervyn Hall wishes PROs would remember.

At 10.30 am the main editorial conference takes place (the *News at One* team has a separate conference at 10.00 am). This is where the flesh is grafted on to the skeleton: updates on stories are discussed by the programme editors, but the conference is also attended by forward planning, senior ITN management, Channel 4 news staff, technical staff, tape libraries, the cuttings department and graphics. ITN's computer-generated graphics are an essential part of many stories, and graphics personnel will talk over exactly what the requirements are for the day. Everyone needs to know what everyone else is doing.

Satellite coordination will also figure in the discussion. If a story needs to be beamed from satellite into the newsroom, the production team will liaise with Eurovision to book time. Eurovision conferences are held three times a day, so news teams can be accommodated quickly.

The news conference is also attended by ITN's associate company, Worldwide Television News. It provides international news-story footage through a worldwide network of film and reporting staff, and its staff too will be able to comment on what footage is available and accessible for the day's news.

By 11.30 am reporters are phoning in with their updates: some stories are about to break; others, which seemed promising, look like damp squibs; two or three stories will run, but much later in the day, so should be moved down the agenda, as editing is likely to be tight. Running orders are amended accordingly.

ITN is buzzing. Production meetings for *News at One* and *News at 5.40 pm* are going on as their schedules are

Surviving the Media Jungle

finally refined, graphics are being produced for *News at Ten*, Mervyn Hall and other editors are keeping abreast of developments in the news.

Special features are being produced too. *News at Ten* has an average of twenty items a day, each of about 1.5 to 2.00 minutes in length, with some fifty-five picture stories per programme. But there are some in-depth features, which also need to be recorded. These will either be on a topical theme or come through the forward planning editor. Such features will be longer (up to 5 minutes), and more focused and analytical than news items. The reporters, scriptwriters and producers of these features will be working on these during the morning.

At 1.00 pm the lunchtime news bulletin goes out, and for the *News at 5.40 pm* and *News at Ten* teams there's a quick lunch break before work resumes. Afternoons pass quickly; there's a great deal to organise. News stories will be recorded and edited, a helicopter is needed at short notice to take a crew to the North of England, and one story will only be ready minutes before going on air (shades of *Broadcast News* again).

There's also the Christie's story on John Lennon's custom-made Mercedes, which is going up for auction. It will make a good closer for the 'and finally . . .' slot – the pictures look great, and the car should make a cool £100,000 at a conservative estimate that afternoon.

As the day progresses, Hall pulls reporters off the stories that will now never make the headlines and sends them off to chase fresher, more promising, bait. News has just come through that pieces of glass have been found in jars of baby food, and it looks like an extortion racket, as more than one manufacturer has suffered. Definitely a lead story!

A DAY IN THE LIFE OF . . .

Hall and his *News at Ten* team watch the news at 5.40 pm and have a production meeting at 6.10 to check on running order and updates. There's another briefing at 7.00 pm. By this time the formal running order for the night's programme is 90 per cent fixed, but a sudden newsflash or crisis will alter it instantly. Most stories are in now, scripted, recorded and edited; but there will be, inevitably, a few latecomers that will arrive when ITN is already on air.

At 9.30 pm the news presenters go into studio for a technical rehearsal. Such rehearsals are essential – apart from reading the script, the presenters need to know which VTR will be played on which machine, which camera will be taking which picture, which graphics will be appearing with which story. There will be two or three stories for which they will write the links, and the rehearsal is the right place for last-minute adjustments to the script. Up in the control room the studio director, writers and producers are watching carefully for any slips.

At 9.55 the familiar – and pre-recorded – tones of Big Ben are mixed with the main headlines. And at 10.00 pm it's on air.

In the control room the director and the team keep an eye out for overrunning and last-minute changes. Some items will be dropped at the last minute, others inserted; but the viewer will never know. That's part of the challenge of live television – no one tuning in would ever suspect the amount of work that goes into making a 30-minute bulletin.

Finally John Lennon's Merc. makes a colourful 45-second closer – bought by an anonymous bidder in Helsinki for £137,500. It's a fun way of ending the pro-

Surviving the Media Jungle

gramme. The news team likes Christie's approach, and has friendly relations with its press office. Sotheby's is good and reliable too.

Of course getting a slot on *News at Ten* is excellent PR for them, but the auction houses know how to handle it. They never ring unless there's a meaty story; they understand what makes grabbing pictures and arresting television; and they realise that it's often better to give crews the facility to film a day or two in advance, rather than take pot luck on the day a story breaks, when crews might be at a premium.

At 10.30 pm Hall and his colleagues can begin to wind down. Time for a beer and a breather. Of course they live off the adrenalin, need the pressure of deadlines. But it's been a long day. ITN's news team hands over to the night news desk and makes its way home. But not in a £137,000 limousine.

3

Enter Grub Street

Statistics show that the average newspaper editor wades through a pile of press releases between 12 and 18 inches high every working day. It may be a hard fact of life for the public relations officer or marketing executive to swallow, but three-quarters of these are binned. The *New York Times* receives around 2 million unsolicited words a day, but it prints only 185,000 from all sources. That's an awful lot of paper going to waste.

Newspaper offices and broadcast newsrooms are never short of bits of paper. They are inundated with news – from their own staff journalists, freelancers, news agencies such as Reuters and the Press Association, and paid-for-by-subscription wire services such as UNS (Universal News Services). Because the media are essentially incestuous, with radio and television following up stories that have first appeared in print, and vice-versa, there's rarely a shortage of good material. Press releases, if you like, are icing on the cake; and more frequently than not they're indigestible.

As we have seen, talk to any journalist about his opinion on the majority of press releases and the same gripes occur again and again:

- Most press releases haven't got a story line.

Surviving the Media Jungle

- Most press releases are boring and long-winded.
- Most press releases are badly written.
- Most press releases arrive after a deadline.
- Most press releases don't target individual media outlets.
- Most writers of press releases don't do their research:

    editors' names are misspelt or out of date, or the releases are addressed to the wrong sections of the publication or programme.

It seems such an easy task to get things right. But according to some of our top journalists, it's a losing battle. We'll look at how to approach radio and television journalists in Chapter 8, as they operate in a slightly different way, but here's just a selection of comments from the world of print.

The industry magazine *PR Week* includes a Spike or Splash column, in which leading newspaper editors gripe or gloat over the week's press releases. It makes interesting reading. 'Editors groan when the day's pile of press releases hits the desk', says Dee Nolan, the former editor of the *Sunday Express Magazine*.

> I've received releases from people who thought I was someone else: the PRO of a well-known margarine company sent me a release addressed to Felicity Lawrence, who, in case you didn't know, was the former editor of the *Sunday Telegraph Magazine*. I've also received an intriguing communiqué from a man who is now a woman, and has set up a venture capital com-

pany to help people 'with gender problems' create their own employment. Appropriately enough, that was addressed to Mr D. Nolan.

Dee Nolan has a sense of humour, but this kind of carelessness is hardly likely to endear her to the PR approach.

Lack of research isn't confined to national publications. Kim Adams, deputy editor of the London Newspaper Group, which publishes fourteen paid and free titles in Central and West London, is also a cynic when it comes to approaches from business and the PR industry:

> Why is it that companies believe that the launch of a new product should be news to a local paper? It might make a trade paper, but it's not news to us. For example, a timber importer wrote to me to outline his firm's restructuring for the 1990s. But his isn't a local firm: what many people don't realise is that if the story is five miles out of a local paper's patch, it might as well be a million miles away.

Kim Adams regularly receives copies of the *Africa Economic Digest, Hong Kong Travel Bulletin* and the glossy Czechoslovak *Life* – all publications, he grins wryly, of the utmost relevance to the residents of Fulham. He cannot undertand why companies don't check to see if the mailing of such material is appropriate. What makes it worse is that the senders never seem to learn their lesson: the same mistakes crop up time and time again.

Apart from the fact that bad targeting – which is what this is – makes bad business sense, it's a highly expensive exercise for the companies concerned. They're wasting valuable money on postage, not to mention executive or secretarial time, sending the wrong material to the wrong publications.

They are also sending this material at the wrong time. According to Jill Churchill, editor of the top-selling magazine *Family Circle*, few press releases understand that consumer magazines such as hers have 6-monthly lead times. In other words, if you want to give *FC* press information about your melt-in-the-mouth brandy Christmas pud, you should be sending it in June. Have you ever wondered why glamorous models are snapped, shivering, and wearing the briefest of bikinis, in the arctic conditions of a typical British winter? For glossies, January probably means August in editorial-speak. Think about it.

Of course timing also means *your* timing. If you know that a story is about to break, get yourself geared for action to notify the press on time.

The press are also turned off by obvious PR stunts, and the kind of blatant letter which begins 'Further to our telephone conversation', when no such conversation has ever taken place. The 'let's try it on' approach is sniffed out by journalists at fifty paces. As Philippa Kennedy, feature writer on the *Daily Express*, once put it: 'I don't mind being approached, but nothing irritates me more than a letter, press release or invitation pressed into a pop-up perfumed flower'.

So – where is all this getting us? Let's go over each point in turn.

Press releases must have a story

Sounds obvious – but as we have seen, many approaches

to the press fail abysmally, because there isn't a storyline to attract the media. Only you can be the judge of that. This means you have to be totally objective; and that's hard, because your company and its products mean a lot to you. You believe in them – if you didn't, you wouldn't be good at your job. Nevertheless, before writing a release or contacting the media, ask yourself the following questions:

- Will this really interest the press?
- Is it telling the newspapers something new, or something they would like to hear?
- Will this information benefit/amuse/interest the paper's readers?

Nine times out of ten it won't. You have to put yourself in the shoes of the journalists who are going to read your press release. How are they going to react? Are they going to shrug their shoulders and say – Big Deal! The Big Deal approach is quite a good litmus test. Try the following:

First, you are the PRO of Longbridge Lawnmowers, and want to publicise the fact that 450,000 lawnmowers were sold last year – an all-time record for Longbridge. Your managing director says he wants this splashed in the national press. Do you have a story?

Be honest. Is this the kind of earth-shattering information that will make the editorial staff of the *Daily Telegraph* hold the front page? Of course not. Big Deal!

Second, you are the PRO of a drugs company which has come up with a cure for baldness. Total hair regrowth occurs over a period of 14 days, and there are no side effects. Your managing director wants national press coverage. Will you get it?

Can you apply the Big Deal test here? No – because what you're talking about has relevance for a great number of people (and probably half of Fleet Street's editors for a start). Baldness can strike anyone at any age. This cure would interest most readers of most publications.

The drug also lends itself to a number of different editorial treatments. If I were a journalist on *The Times*, say, I would probably write a short and serious paragraph about the cure, and it might be sandwiched at the bottom of page 4, if it were a light news-day, or more probably in the medical column. But if I were writing for a more popular newspaper, such as the *Daily Mail* or the *Daily Express*, I would turn the cure for baldness into a light-hearted feature. I'd probably get celebrity 'baldies' such as Clive James or Gordon Honeycombe to try the drug out, and photograph the results. But whichever way you look at it, this cure is news.

The more widely you read, the more you get to know newspapers' and magazines' house styles – the kinds of stories they publish – and the better you will recognise whether you have a story for them or not. It takes time, and patience – but it's worth it.

Press releases must be sent to the right publication

Let's look at Longbridge Lawnmowers again. The sale of 450,000 lawnmowers is not news of national importance.

ENTER GRUB STREET

But who would find this kind of information relevant or useful? Refer back to Chapter 1 and look at the way media lists are compiled. Check your list, and, alongside this list, write down the reasons you think the publications or programmes would be interested. In the case of Longbridge such a list would probably look something like this:

1 Lawnmower/electrical goods trade press, e.g. *Electrical and Retail Trader* – Longbridge will want to tell the opposition how well it's doing, and impress on shops how it has boosted their sales figures and profits.

2 Hardware/DIY press, e.g. *DIY Monthly* – especially if the Longbridge lawnmower is available at these outlets.

3 Gardening press, e.g. *Gardeners World* magazine – how does Longbridge's compare in sales to other lawnmowers? What are the benefits of this mower to gardeners?

4 Consumer publications, e.g. *House & Garden* – also encompasses certain special interest publications such as *You and Your Barclaycard*, whose readership would be interested.

5 Local papers – Longbridge must have a factory somewhere. Have these record sales figures meant a boost in local employment?

6 Local freesheets – along with local weekly and evening papers, these are useful outlets for press information.

Surviving the Media Jungle

7 Local radio – both BBC and ILR radio stations would be interested in a 'local firm makes good' story.

8 Local TV, BBC or Independent – here apply the Big Deal test. Television, even local television, is notoriously difficult to get into. But if there's a really good regional story . . .

9 National BBC/ILR gardening programmes – radio.

10 National BBC/Independent gardening programmes – television.

Neither the national radio or TV programmes may use this item, but they will probably keep it as useful background information for their files – and, you never know, may well contact Longbridge if they are considering doing a feature on lawnmowers in future editions.

As you can see, even though Longbridge hasn't made the front page of the *Financial Times*, there are still enough media outlets to get the variety of coverage the managing director is asking for. Managing directors are always trying to get into the *Financial Times*, and sometimes they will. Often, however, their desire for a splash in the *FT* is conditioned solely by ego.

The *FT* is the newspaper most company directors read, so that a feature in the *FT* is likely to impress the MD's peers. There is nothing wrong in this, but I would argue that satisfying an MD's ego is not a sufficient business reason to pursue coverage in the *Financial Times*. In this case the fact that 450,000 lawnmowers have been sold isn't news *à la FT* unless Longbridge can come up with a few more interesting angles – we'll come to angles or news hooks in Chapter 4.

Local newspapers are greatly undervalued. They build up strong loyalties among their readers, and serve a definite regional need. A recent survey showed that, faced with a choice of giving up their evening local paper or their national daily newspaper, 60 per cent of readers would opt to keep the regional paper.

Local newspapers are marvellous hunting grounds for the publicity-conscious company, keen to promote itself to potential customers – and of course potential employees. People love to read about local firms and local people doing well *locally*. Regional Englishness is alive and well. Some might call it xenophobia, but it's probably why we won the war. Local radio and television programmes serve exactly the same purpose.

I've left the trade press till last, because when it comes to trade publications, you're home and dry. Of course your trade magazine will want to hear about your company: that's why it's in business. Coverage in the trade press should not be ignored, and it's probably the easiest to achieve.

Unless your company has somehow managed to alienate press and/or public opinion in the past, your news should be good news for trade magazines. If you don't know what your trade publications are, look up a directory like *PIMS, Willings Press Guide*, or *PNA* (see Appendix I, p. 201). You'll find all sorts of weird and wonderful publications. There's the *Undertakers Gazette, Crematorium Monthly, Mortality and Morbidity Weekly* – as well as *Hotel and Catering Monthly* and *Cash and Carry Wholesaler*.

If a business exists, you'll find a trade magazine supporting it. Some publications, such as *The Lepidopterist* or *Zerb* (the magazine for film and TV cameramen), only appear three times a year and are run by dedicated enthusiasts who put the magazine together in their spare time. They may not have the cash or clout of the IPC group or Condé Nast, but even these publications have uncovered a 'niche readership' that may very well be of use to your business. Don't discount them.

Press releases must be sent to the right person

It's not just a question of spelling the editor's name correctly, although it's vital to do so. It's also a question of sending your release to the right person anyway. Dee Nolan's story is quite a typical one: the mailing list of many a public relations company is often hopelessly out of date. It's important to update your mailing list every 6 months, and even though directories are a useful aid, they should never be relied on exclusively.

There's only one way to ensure you're sending your releases to the right people – and that, I'm afraid, is an old-fashioned ring-round. It takes time and it's boring, and if you've got a list of several hundred names, you'll be gnashing your teeth after the first hour. But it works.

Many people, PROs and businessmen alike, make the mistake of thinking that the person you should be sending releases to is the editor. That is rarely the case. You might get away with it on a trade or local newspaper, because the editorial team is usually small and staff journalists often double up: the reporter who writes the woman's page may also cover local politics and the TV page. But national newspapers and magazines are very different animals. If you think about the editor's role, it's very similar to that of a company chairman. The chairmen are responsible for the strategy of a company, global growth and corporate objectives, but they probably won't have a hands-on approach to the business.

Newspaper and magazine editors are the same: they're concerned with the look of the publication, its total content, its ratio of editorial to advertising, its sales figures and forecasts, but they will probably not play a part in the day-to-day selection of material. That's the job of the individual section editors. These are the journalists whose job it is to fill the pages, and you have to convince them you have a story.

Flick through the pages of any magazine or newspaper. There are science and technology editors, features editors, diary editors, news editors, political editors, picture editors, financial and business editors – the list is endless. Each knows his patch. You should know theirs. Think about your story and target it. Is it a science story? Could it even interest more than one section of the paper?

A few years ago, when cable and satellite television first hit the headlines, I was working for the public relations firm Burson-Marsteller. We were asked to publicise the launch of the first square satellite dish or Squarial, made by the Japanese company Matsushita.

It was obvious that the trade press – such magazines as *Broadcast* and *Televisual* – would be interested in this development. But we were particularly keen to reach the national press. The story, as we saw it, was two-pronged: it had obvious technological interest, but it was also a story about the growth of satellite television – a media story. So we sent press releases to both the science and the media correspondents of the national newspapers. All printed it, on different days and in different sections of the paper. The targeting worked.

But don't get carried away. Even if your story has more than two angles, there's no point bombarding section editors with press releases: two is quite enough. You just have to use your imagination and your common sense. Targeting is one thing, but you don't want journalists taking one look at your press release and thinking: 'Oh Lord, another release from XXX. And who's he sent it to this time?' Selecting the journalists you send material to is an important part of media relations, and should be handled with care. It's all part of being a professional.

Press releases must be sent at the right time

That means never after a deadline. The worst thing you can do is to send a journalist copy when he no longer needs it. News is transient. Reporters' desks on the *Daily Express* are cleared by cleaners every night. If there are sheets of paper, and half-written articles still on the typewriter – too bad. It all gets thrown away. There will be other stories tomorrow. James Cameron, perhaps one of this century's most distinguished newsmen, used to say that whenever he met journalists bragging about the campaigning role of the press in changing social attitudes, he quietly reminded them that the Greek word for a journalist is *ephemeridis* – a dealer in ephemera. News is the most ephemeral product of all.

ENTER GRUB STREET

So make sure your stories and releases reach their targets on time. If you want to know when to send material to the press, you can always phone up and ask. But here are some rules of thumb. We have already seen that glossy magazines such as *Family Circle* need their material at least 6 months in advance; national and local papers are less demanding:

- National dailies, even with today's 24-hour printing technology. shouldn't be contacted later than 4.30 pm if you want a story in the following day. Naturally crises are the exception. (Crises are always the exception.)

- Local evening papers, such as the *Standard* or *Manchester Evening News*, should not be contacted later than 12.30 pm for inclusion in that day's edition, and preferably before 11.00 am.

- Weekly papers should be contacted the week before they go to press – in other words, if your local weekly comes out on a Thursday and goes to press on a Wednesday, it should not be contacted later than Tuesday.

- Sunday colour supplements, like glossy consumer magazines, have fairly long lead times too – the average is about 3 months. So if you want to send them details about a gorgeously expensive and calorific box of Valentine's Day chocolate truffles, guaranteed to brighten and fatten some lucky girl's 14 February, you should consider doing so in November.

Surviving the Media Jungle

There are a few other tips which can help you sell your stories better. Never contact a Sunday paper on a Monday – that's the editorial team's well-earned day off. On the other hand, Mondays are notoriously quite days for news, so the clued-up PRO may well get a Monday morning splash for his client by contacting a national daily on Saturday or Sunday.

One thing that should be remembered is that the telephone is perhaps your best asset. Use it. Press releases and letters can be binned – phone calls can't. Phone up journalists and introduce yourself, explain whom you represent. Ask them what stories they want, and whether they have a schedule of forthcoming features that can be sent to you. Cultivate the relationship. Don't offer lunch for the sake of it, but suggest meeting for a drink so you can get to know what the journalists need. You'll soon find that if you come across as honest, forthright, aware of the way they operate and accessible, and if you treat them with the kind of professional respect they like to think they deserve, you will be forming the basis of good press relations.

If you've obeyed all the rules, there's no reason why you shouldn't get your story into print. After all, you've studied the newspaper, got a 'feel' for the story, targeted the journalist correctly and mailed it on time. There's only one thing that might stop you, the one thing you can never foresee or predict, and which prevents even the best PR stories from being printed – a national or international crisis.

No one can know when a disaster, will ocur. It could be earthquakes in Armenia, a rail tragedy in Clapham, or a chemical explosion in Bhopal. If a crisis does happen, it's more than likely you can kiss your story goodbye.

There probably won't be room for it in the paper because of the extended coverage such crises produce.

If you're lucky, you might find your story will be picked up a few days later; that can happen if it's 'evergreen'. You can also telephone the journalist and politely remind him of your story's existence. It might work. But you will probably find that you'll be spiked through no fault of your own. A crisis encapsulates the lottery that is media relations. You can never be sure your story will win through; there's always something that can go wrong. But at least you've done your best.

4

Fishing for angles

The editor of the *Sun* is quoted as saying that any story containing the words 'free', 'sex', or 'win' would have every chance of making the first edition. In fact, a press release with the title 'WIN FREE SEX!' would be guaranteed publication. That's the kind of headline the *Sun*'s 4 million readers like to see in their daily paper.

On a more parochial note, the *Preston Bury Times* carried a story about one Vivienne Eastwood, who lives in Preston, and who was thankfully *not* injured in the Clapham rail tragedy. A perfect reason for printing a story, you may think, until you read the piece again. It transpires that Mrs Eastwood was going to London and *would have been*, at her own estimation, on the very train that crashed if flu hadn't prevented her from travelling that day. If you think the rationale is spurious, you're probably right – but the angle was perfect for a local paper. Mrs Eastwood and her lucky escape made the front page.

The press prints the news it wants to print, and if it likes the look of a story, it will even angle it into a newsworthy item when there's little substance to back it up. Mrs Eastwood is just one example. The Pamella Bordes affair was another. You may remember this was the case of a former Miss India who was given a House of

Surviving the Media Jungle

Commons pass. On the face of it Miss Bordes was working as a 'researcher', and it was only Miss Bordes' lack of qualifications and her dubious professionalism that gave rise to questions in the House about the frequency with which such passes were issued, and to whom.

If Miss Bordes had looked like the back of a bus, the story would probably have been relegated to the middle pages of the broadsheets, and totally ignored by the tabloids. As it was, pictures of the nubile and voluptuous Miss Bordes graced the pages of every newspaper from *The Times* to the *Sun*. The original story-angle, 'How had this bimbo got a researcher's pass?', was totally forgotten. Instead the public was treated to more forbidden fruit: newspaper and broadcast reports wallowed in Miss Bordes' connections with rich and famous men, her associations with Libya, and her dreams and aspirations of becoming a film star.

The fact that the whole business seems to have been a carefully plotted public relations stunt on Miss Bordes' behalf shows how a strategic 'angle' can change the direction of press coverage. No one comes out well in the affair: the press is seen as gullible, and it is an example of a press relations campaign of the worst type. But there's no doubt that it worked.

Most campaigns will not, fortunately, have to resort to these sorts of tactics, but angles are a vital part of any story. They are particularly important when you are stumped for ideas about publicising something, and wish to create news when there is no news. A novel slant to your company's product or service may often be all you need to generate a healthy crop of cuttings.

I'm assuming that your product or service is actually

worthy of mention here, and that all you need is a gentle push. Obviously there is no point desperately trying to publicise a product that is clearly not worth the effort.

News about recent professional appointments, your company's relocation to new headquarters and winners of competitions (unless it's the Pools) are unlikely to make the front page of *The Times*. You should confine these items to your trade or local news outlets, where they belong. Nor is the fact that you have advertised in a paper or magazine enough reason to expect you will be given editorial gratis. Like a good marriage, editorial has to be worked at.

Having studied newspapers and broadcast reports in some depth, I've come up with a **fourteen-point plan** which, if followed to the letter, is guaranteed to give you coverage. Every story that ever made the headlines will obey one or more of the following headings. Just look at what you're publicising, mix and match, and take your pick.

1 Surveys

News editors love surveys. Flick through any paper, tabloid or broadsheet, listen to any radio report, view any TV bulletin, and you will find surveys making the news. They can be specially commissioned, well-researched polls by MARPLAN or MORI, or 'quick and dirty' surveys you can prepare yourself: simply go out on to the street and ask a representative 100 or so individuals selected questions that will get your product mentioned. It doesn't seem to matter how authoritative

Surviving the Media Jungle

the survey is, it's just the sort of useful 'filler' that is picked on by the press for the 'nibs' – or news-in-brief paragraphs you find in newspapers such as the *Daily Mail*.

Public relations consultant Michael Bland publishes a twice-yearly guide to the PR campaigns that have succeeded in obtaining coverage in the print media, and analyses the reasons why. (In fact I worked with him to research and write the first guide, which was published in 1987.) He maintains that *twice as many stories are generated by surveys than by any other means*. It's worth thinking about next time you plan a campaign.

Surveys can be about anything. They can be studious 'How many people own their own homes' surveys, or light-hearted and frivolous. A manufacturer of men's underpants commissioned a survey to find out how many pairs of briefs the average British male had in his wardrobe: twelve, apparently, giving lie to the saying 'one on, one off, and one in the wash!'

In 1988, which was a leap year, romantic fiction publishers Silhouette asked 1,000 young men whether they would answer 'I do' if their girl friends proposed. The answer was unequivocal: girls were assured of a 98 per cent success rate. The results were published on 14 February, St Valentine's Day, which was a clever piece of targeting.

Insurance company Legal and General ran a survey to find out how much a housewife thought she was worth if she were paid the going rate for the job, and came up with the sum of £15,000 (about the salary of a middle-ranking PR account handler). This was all good PR for Legal and General, and also good PR for its new life assurance scheme, which was specifically aimed at women.

2 Award schemes

This is another excellent way of generating coverage. Ally your company to a worthwhile scheme, and you can only enhance your business reputation. The press, which may resist the kind of obvious PR approach we've discussed earlier, will also be more willing to co-operate and give you coverage if you're not just lining your own pockets but helping someone else.

The National Dairy Council, for instance, sponsors the Milk Cup Athletics Championships, the breeding ground of our best and brightest atheletes.

One example of an award scheme that worked, and which generated a great deal of coverage for the sponsor, is the Trusthouse Forte Community Chest. Here the Conservation Foundation, which was founded by David Bellamy and concentrates on linking big business to conservation, joined forces with THF to create the Community Chest, an award of up to £1,500 a month to worthwhile conservation projects anywhere in the British Isles. David Bellamy and a bevy of celebrity judges, including Susan Hampshire, met each month to choose the winning entries.

Local managers of THF inns, hotels and motorway service areas were encouraged to adopt their local winning schemes and see them through. The winners were a marvellously mixed bunch. They included a little old lady in Scotland, who was awarded £200 to help her catalogue wild flowers that grew along the motorway; the owner of a pair of Napoleonic flags, who used his prize money to restore them to their former glory; and Les and Sue Stocker from Aylesbury, well-known for their animal hospital, who set up the St Tiggywinkles

Hedgehog Hospital in their back garden as a result of a win through the Community Chest.

The Stockers obtained national print and television coverage when St Tiggywinkles opened its doors – it seemed that the whole of Fleet Street had crowded into the tiny back garden on their housing estate. The lawn was knee-deep in photographers and camera crews craning to get a shot of Susan Hampshire holding one poor prickly wounded beastie.

From a PR point of view the national news coverage obtained was good for THF, but in fact most of the Community Chest press coverage was local news, and that was the strategy behind the scheme. Regional coverage has a snowball effect: before too long the message 'THF cares about the environment' spread from local to national news, which was precisely the point. The award scheme had succeeded in its objective of creating a humane face for a large, amorphous hotel and catering group.

If this comes across as hard-boiled, it's not meant to be. There's no reason why big business shouldn't work with small, deserving groups for mutual benefit. David Bellamy calls it 'Symbio-tech', the happy union of sound commercialism and social conscience. It might sound cynical – but it works.

3 Media events

Many people still believe that a media event is a public relations stunt, complete with frilly blondes bursting out of giant iced cakes. That's rather an old-fashioned view, and thankfully disappearing. Gin and tonic is a popular aperitif, but it's not the only staple tipple of PR practitioners.

A properly stage-managed media event is an excellent vehicle for coverage, but it must be part of a well thought-out media relations campaign: there's no room for inspired but chaotically unscheduled afterthoughts. Media events offer business opportunities, as well as press liaison, and need to be treated seriously.

One of the most dramatic media events over the last few years was Australia's Bicentenary. To coincide with Australia's 200th birthday celebrations, there were exhibitions, arts festivals and trade fairs in every state; and many of these events were co-ordinated overseas, bringing a touch of Oz to Europe and North America.

The media coverage that ensued was phenomenal, proving that Australia was at the forefront of science and technology, and certainly not the arid cultural desert typified by such films as *Crocodile Dundee*. The French Revolution's bicentenary celebrations similarly did wonders for France.

On a smaller scale the launch of the Astra TV satellite in late 1988, which effectively brought DBS (direct broadcasting by satellite) television within reach of the average consumer, was an excellent opportunity to stage a conference called 'What is Satellite TV?' The conference aimed to explain the mysteries of the new technology to the press, and was well-attended by the media. Representatives of national broadsheets, tabloids, radio and television found the conference useful and informative, and they left well-briefed. It was also very good PR for British Telecom International, which holds the licence for Astra.

Surviving the Media Jungle

A media event can be an exhibition, trade fair, conference or press conference (we'll discuss the use and abuse of press conferences in Chapter 7). To succeed, it must be linked to a news peg such as an anniversary or special event. In some cases the very fact of launching a new product on to the market can be the trigger, but be warned – journalists are not going to invest several hours of their precious time coming to a new product 'do' unless a very tasty carrot is dangled in front of their eyes.

One such carrot was the launch of the margarine Delight! This product was positioned in the market place as the margarine for the outdoor life. Its target consumer was typically young, affluent, sporty. Picking up on this theme, the launchers of the product flew journalists by helicopter to an exclusive health and fitness centre, where they were able to try out sports such as hanggliding, parachute jumping and wind-surfing, as well as feasting on sandwiches spread with Delight! margarine. It was one of the most successful events ever staged, and the press was clamouring for invitations. Naturally you need a client with a big PR budget for this sort of media splash, but it obeys the golden rule: give the press something it wants, and it will be good to you.

But sometimes stagey media bashes like these can go wrong, and that's the danger. The launch of a well-known insect repellent was one example. The PR company was desperate to find an attractive angle with which to bait the press, and the thought of publicising an insect repellent was hardly a stimulating prospect. The team hit on the idea of inviting a well-known television fitness expert to try the product out. Dressed only in a swimsuit, the brave lady was to smear herself with the repellent and enter a cage holding 1,000 starving female mosquitoes. She was to stay in the cage for 5 minutes and emerge unmolested. She agreed, having first negotiated a hefty fee.

Journalists swarmed to the launch. The prospect of this lady in a swimsuit facing 1,000 winged syringes had created quite a buzz at El Vino's. As each reporter arrived, he was given a press pack containing product information and a free sample. Which was just as well, for when our intrepid adventuress went into the cage, something went wrong with the latch – and the mosquitoes escaped! As one they zoomed in on the press corps. Much sweating and swatting in the ranks. Never have free samples been used with such speed. The press had plastered themselves in the cream before you could say 'Quinine'.

The next day every newspaper had a picure story of the event, some with a blithely smiling and totally unbitten TV star. 'BITING BACK AT THE PRESS!' was a favoured headline, and the reports went on to say that the cream was indeed an effective repellent: few of the journalists had suffered as a result of their little contretemps with Anopheles.

The PR team was lucky: the press had seen the funny side, and treated the story accordingly. But it was a risk. Unfavourable reports could have killed the product before it reached the shops. And though they swear that the incident happened by accident, rather than by design, I wonder. Many a PRO has dreamed of getting his own back on a group of hapless hacks, and what better way to do it than via a product launch?

4 Charity

As for the award scheme, linking your company or product with a charity is good news. It demonstrates the value of a *shared story*: both you and the charity get coverage.

Premier Brands manufacture the low-fat milk powder Marvel, and Marvel have sponsored the British Heart Foundation's 'Slim and Save Lives Campaign'. Fatties from all over the UK go on sponsored diets, and for every pound of weight that they lose, money is donated to research into heart disease.

The person who loses more weight than anyone else wins a glamorous holiday for two in some exotic location, and a high-street store donates a clothing voucher so that the winner can stock up on the newest fashions to suit his or her slim-line figure. Thousands of entrants slim to save lives every year, and it has been a major part of Marvel's PR campaign. The coverage gained is always extensive.

The charity doesn't have to be a large national concern. Local charities can link up very successfully with local businesses. The beauty is that everybody benefits.

5 Opportunity PR

I was one of the unfortunate Kentish dwellers who lost her roof during the terrible hurricane in October 1987. My husband and I covered the gaping maw with tarpaulin and plastic sheeting, and thumbed through *Yellow Pages* for a roofer. After fifteen calls it became clear that roofers were at a premium. Their job-sheets were chock-a-block, and the majority were charging exorbitant prices. They were cashing in on others' misfortunes.

So many people were in exactly the same predicament that we faced the prospect of weeks, if not months, without a proper roof. In the meantime the weather became very wet, and we had buckets all over the house; water was seeping into the one good Persian carpet in the drawing room, and the dog was whining piteously.

Cooking is one of my hobbies, and I often cook when I get depressed, because preparing food is such a blissfully concentrating activity: all you have to worry about is the dish in front of you, and you can be creative with little intellectual effort. The lack of a roof over my head made me extremely depressed, and as I was preparing some cheering recipe, I turned on the radio and tuned into a phone-in programme.

'My name's Bill Johnson', I heard, 'and I'd like to say that there's a lot of people being ripped off with this hurricane business. I'm a roofer, I'm looking for work, and if anyone wants to give me a ring, I can guarantee them a professional job, well finished, and at a good price.' Within seconds I had dialled his number. Bill Johnson lived nearly 20 miles away, but he came round that afternoon, gave me a fair estimate, and did a super job. He probably wasn't aware of it, but that's opportunity PR.

After the Clapham rail disaster a nearby cafeteria supplied tea and sandwiches round the clock to the medical team, firemen and police who were helping the injured. The goodwill that this created made for excellent public relations. I'm not suggesting that this is the reason the gesture was made, but I know which cafeteria I would go to if I were in the area and wanted a bite to eat. The local paper followed the story through with a profile of the owner and his wife, and no doubt that coverage helped their business. It deserved to.

Opportunity PR isn't confined to helping out in disasters. It's a question of looking around you and grabbing the chance to make your company shine. Often opportunity PR is allied to what's in the news, so keep your eyes peeled for titbits. The secret lies in lateral thinking.

6 Children and animals

They say you should never work with children or animals on stage, but in PR terms you're on to a winner. Think of the Miss Pears beauty competition: every year some smiling ringleted little girl achieves her 15 minutes of stardom, and all because Pears Soap, in the long-distant past, came up with a brilliant PR idea. Miss Pears is an example of how mixed headings under the fourteen-point plan can work:

- it's a media event,
- an award scheme,
- working with children.

.It can't fail. And it doesn't.

The 'aah-isn't-he-sweet' factor, when it comes to either children or animals, has been well exploited by advertising agencies. When you next watch the news on

ITN, count the number of commercials during the break employing two tiny or four floppy feet. It's quite a significant proportion. Duke the Dulux Dog and Arthur the White Cat are media superstars, and it's no coincidence that the most popular commercial ever made was for Andrex toilet paper, featuring those lovable roly-poly Labrador pups.

For the PRO with imagination, children and animals are an excellent way of demonstrating a product. A toddler could be taught to operate a computer, to show how easy it is to use. (This would also make a striking PR pic – see Chapter 6.)

When Spillers launched their Prime dogfood, set at a premium price, they organized a 'Top Dog Photo-call'. A selection of Britain's pedigree pooches were invited to the Ritz for a slap-up dinner of Winalot Prime. Complete with officious waiter, silver service, napkins tucked under their whiskers, the dogs were photographed at table, looking extremely regal. The shot must have taken hours to set up, but it was a beauty. It was featured by nearly every tabloid and a healthy smattering of broadsheets. It also shows how useful a touch of humour can be in selling a story to the press.

7 Sex and age

Newspaper headlines over the last few years have convinced the average reader that all you need to do to get immediate press coverage is to uncover as much of your body as possible. This may be true, but it is hardly the kind of coverage that lasts. Who now remembers Erica

Surviving the Media Jungle

Roe, who once streaked across a football pitch? Who remembers the faces, let alone the names, of the page 3 girls in the *Star*? One pair of 38-D cups is very much like another. Blondes draped across the bonnets of cars are a yawn, and alienate the female consumer. Gradually marketing men are beginning to realise that sex sells scandal, not product.

However, replace the word 'sex' by 'gender', and you are immediately entering the realistic world of press relations.

The first woman astronaut, supersonic pilot, director of a public limited company – all this makes news. The winner of the Veuve Clicquot Businesswoman of the Year competition is guaranteed publicity: just think of Sophie Mirman and Sock Shop. And since this is a book about equal opportunities, the same applies to men. The first man to do an unusual, difficult or hazardous job/feat/stunt/sport . . . or anything else will be the person the newsmen will want to talk about.

The oldest person to do something is also a good news banker. Everyone remembers the media coverage obtained by the 80-year-old grandmother who wanted to fly in Concorde. The oldest person ever to obtain an Open University degree was another media winner. 'Gold watch' ceremonies may be useful for keeping your firm in the news for local press.

8 Health and safety

If the chemist Sir Humphry Davey had invented the miner's safety lamp today, he would have been astounded by the number of newspaper, radio and television programmes wanting to cover the story. Health and safety are matters of universal concern.

The first company to introduce flame-proof furniture foam, after the spate of fires that showed domestic foam-filled sofas and chairs to be fire hazards, was assured of favourable national publicity. Companies that kept to the old, unsafe foam received damaging press coverage.

Campaigning television programmes, such as *That's Life!* are always itching to get their hands on a health and safety topic, and, as we've seen, bad news for your company is good news for TV. Averting this kind of probing inquiry is a matter for preparedness planning, and it's important to recognise the press's hunger for potentially controversial issues.

Salmonella in eggs and listeria in cheese are just two national scares that have broken in the past few years. It's always best to be aware of the potentially negative issue, so that it can be skilfully averted or at the very least contained. That's not media white-washing, it's crisis management.

On the other hand, if you have good news, share it. If a cure for AIDS is found, the pharmaceutical company that produces it will receive international acclaim. Such topics touch the nerves of a nation. They are more than news stories; in their own way they enter the history books.

9 Environment

Our planet has become the hot issue of the 1990s. Ever

Surviving the Media Jungle

since the greening of Mrs Thatcher, words like 'ozone-layer' and 'tropical rain-forest' have tripped off the tongue of the man in the street. Groups such as Friends of the Earth, which perhaps in the 1970s were considered to be amiable freaks, overnight turned into spokemen for the world. Being green, and, more importantly, being seen to be green, has become politically and socially fashionable.

As a writer and broadcaster on conservation issues, I look on this sudden explosion of conscience with wry amusement and a degree of concern. It would be comforting to think that the green issue has at last embedded itself in the political infrastructure, but I worry that it may soon be swept away by the next popular hobby-horse. However, wearing my marketing hat, I find the environment offers many opportunities for creative press relations.

Trusthouse Forte's Community Chest scheme, as we have seen, was just one example of symbio-technology. Metal Box had another, when it developed the first aerosol in this country to be powered by ozone-friendly propellant – not a CFC in sight. Gillette actively sponsored MB in this task – it wanted an environmentally suitable shaving foam developed – and the media coverage that resulted was good for Gillette, good for Metal Box, and even helped the ozone layer too.

Anita Roddick, head of the Body Shop group, is also doing her bit. She has launched a campaign to 'Stop the Burning' of Brazilian rainforests by selling T-shirts, and giving out posters and leaflets in her stores urging customers to write to the Brazilian government and protest. I'd call that good PR.

10 Special days/milestones

When Terry's of York celebrated 200 years of confectionery-making, the public relations team immediately planned a series of media-related events, both national and local. *The Times*'s bicentenary also gave rise to celebrations, special birthday editions, and even a television documentary about the rise of the Thunderer.

Anniversaries make good news pegs. In order to find out what special days are coming up, look at such reference books as *Conference and Exhibitions Monthly*, the *Writers' and Artists' Yearbook* and the *UK Press Gazette*. All of these feature pages of diary events, some of which could trigger off ideas for your company.

Significant numbers make good media triggers too. The millionth customer to walk into a department store, the icing of the thousandth Christmas cake – both could be made into a story, or a picture story. If you can truly say, with your hand on your heart, that the product you produce is honest-to-goodness unique, unusual, of genuine consumer interest, and has never been thought of before, you're likely to interest the press.

11 Eccentrics

The Brits love eccentrics. Sadly the number of genuine eccentrics seems to be diminishing, but if you know of someone who is the genuine article, and if you can persuade him to endorse or ally himself in some way to your company, you are halfway to achieving novel and entertaining press coverage.

It's the old story: 'Dog bites man' isn't news, 'Man

bites dog' is news. Does your eccentric have an unusual or interesting hobby? A collector of antique lavatory chains, bathtubs and sinks was successfully employed by one leading bathroom manufacturer to emphasise the change over the years from the downright basic to the hedonistically luxurious.

One bicycle company recreated a Penny-farthing bicycle race, and assembled a clutch of one-wheel bikers – most of them over sixty – to ride across Rotten Row. The sight of superannuated Hell's Angels, complete with metal-studded jackets, flying across Kensington Gardens was highly entertaining, and the event was filmed by Thames News, the after-six local news programme. It made good television.

12 Personalities

Closely allied to eccentrics are personalities (who can be one and the same). To use a celeb or not to use a celeb is a question frequently asked among the PR fraternity. The answer is simple: *use a celebrity if he/she will enhance your company message and not overshadow your product.* You may recall the Joan Collins/Leonard Rossiter advertisements, in which Mr Rossiter spilled a drink down the front of La Collins' cleavage. Everyone remembers the advertisement, but few remember the name of the product that was being endorsed. (It was Cinzano.)

Don't use a personality just for the sake of it. Celebrities can prove expensive – a fee of several thousand pounds an hour is not unusual – and can be temperamental. Often lesser lights – up and coming sportsmen, a local dignitary or MP, a well-known local businessman, a popular regional disc-jockey – are just as appropriate.

If you do decide to use a celebrity, he/she should also be specially targeted to fit in with your marketing plans, and suit the company image. There's no point having Linda Lusardi, the former page 3 girl, endorsing surgical stockings, when fishnet tights might be more appropriate.

Well-chosen, celebrities can fulfil the important function of getting the press there, and creating photo opportunities, but they should never be the sole rationale behind the exercise. The product must be able to stand alone and speak for itself, or you'll have problems.

13   Piggy-backs

Shared stories are examples of piggy-backing on other companies or products for news, and the Marvel/British Heart Foundation link-up is typical. Several manufacturers of camera equipment, for example, could join forces to sell-in a feature on the latest photographic developments.

PROs and PR companies don't pay enough attention to shared stories, and I believe they are wasting many a good opportunity by unconscious protectionism. Clients are to blame too: they become so over-protective of *their* product, *their* story, that it doesn't occur to them to share the limelight so that everybody can benefit. It is also easier to sell a shared story to the media than one single PR plug.

Surviving the Media Jungle

In fact journalists covering a feature on cameras will probably share the story anyway, parcelling the feature up between three or four different products. By pre-empting them you're actually saving the journalist work.

Piggy-backs can also be created by jumping on to a topical news item and allying it to your company. The year *1992* is a perfect example of how PROs representing many different facets of industry have placed features in the press discussing their company's plans to operate in the single European market.

The fashion industry has also piggy-backed on vogue films and theatrical events. The film *Out of Africa* gave rise to a rash of safari suits in the shops, with attendant media coverage, and the media's rediscovery of the early 1960s, with such films as *Scandal* and *Dance with a Stranger*, has resulted in fashion going backwards to the heyday of the Beatles.

Piggy-backs are useful and under-used media tools. Don't forget them.

14 Pictures

It's a truism that 'a picture paints a 1,000 words', and in PR terms nothing succeeds so much as a strong and interesting pic. Photography will be covered in-depth in Chapter 6, but I'll leave you with the thought that Susan Hampshire cuddling a bandaged hedgehog made the pages of the *Daily Express* and the *Guardian* (as well as ITN's 'and finally' slot).

As we have seen, the big auction houses, such as Sotheby's and Christie's, regularly get coverage with shots of unusual objets d'art coming up for sale. The more original or unusual the photograph, the more likely it will be taken up and used.

Angles are the news-hooks and pegs of any story. Create the right angle and you're halfway home.

5

How to write a press release

The common-or-garden press release may well be the quickest and simplest way of supplying information to the press, but, as the previous chapters show, many executives fall at the first hurdle. Their releases just don't stand up to the needs of Fleet Street.

Part of the problem is that everyone thinks they can write, and a popular misconception amongst the business fraternity is that just because you're good at marketing, or excel in financial affairs, you are automatically a good writer. Not so, as Fleet Street knows to its cost. There is little difference between a release and junk mail: both are unsolicited and have to be pretty good – or they'll be chucked.

We've seen what editors are looking for: short, sharp copy, which tells the story concisely, without puffery. They want interesting material, with bright newsy angles that will make their readers say 'Well, what do you know!' They do not need over-long boring press releases about me-too products, which have been written simply to please the managing director of Widgets Unlimited.

What do I mean by this? It's easier to show by example than to theorise. My thanks here go to the many editors and features editors of national newspapers who hap-

Surviving the Media Jungle

Press release 1

THE UP-TO-THE MINUTE IT SERVICE

[3] **Communications will take a giant step forward** next week when a new IT service becomes available to British commerce and industry.

[3] **Forging ahead of all its rivals in the field**, Britain's Computech Ltd., a top computer systems and communications company, has launched the up-to-the minute information management service: Retrieve.

[2] Retrieve is **a unique one-stop information, communication and transaction facility**. It enables instant access to a company's entire base of supplier and client contacts and information sources on a world-wide basis. It is now available
[2] to companies in the UK for the first time. In addition, **over 1,200 external information databases are linked into the service.**

[4] Providing low-cost access to the largest set of private and public data bases in the world, **Retrieve has already been described as the world's most advanced service.**

... more/2

'Even the non-technical company executive will be able to use the unique facilities with just ten minutes of introduction' says John Uppingham, Computech's Managing Director.

[5] Retrieve will provide **near-instant access to City Reports, World-wide Press Comment, Company Information, Technical and Scientific Research and much more**
[6] **besides** – fully integrated with the client's own internal systems.

[7] Issued on behalf of: Nu-Tech PR Ltd.
32 Forest Gate, London SW3
Tel: 01 402 4156

pily jumped in and sent me the worst examples of press releases they could find! The following releases have had the names of the products and personalities changed, to protect the innocent (or guilty, depending on your point of view) but have otherwise been reproduced *in esse*.

Both were sent to the features editor of a national daily newspaper, who has asked not to be named but who has passed his comments on to me. They both exhibit the most common PR faults: a zealous tendency to exaggerate the merits of the product, over-extravagant claims, carelessness and sloppy writing, and jargon for jargon's sake, rendering the whole useless and quite unprintable.

Critique

The release has several fundamental errors:

1 It was sent to the features editor of a national newspaper – why? This is a business/high-tech story, and should have been targeted accordingly.
2 It doesn't explain how the system works: the layman will not understand what a 'unique one-stop information, communication and transaction facility' is. This is jargon of the worst type, and should be put into language normal people understand. To make it even clearer, an example should be given, especially as 1,200 databases can be allegedly accessed by the system: e.g. 'At the touch of a button, Retrieve will access your clients and supplier databases, nationally and world-wide. The system can also be linked to other marketing and information sources, such as Prestel'.
3 It glories in its clichés: 'Communications will take a

Surviving the Media Jungle

giant step forward', 'Forging ahead of all its rivals in the field', 'a unique . . . facility'. Editors don't look too kindly on such claims to fame. Just tell the truth, the whole truth and nothing but the truth.

4   Retrieve has already been described as the world's most advanced service: by whom? If you're going to go over the top, you should credit a source.
5   Why are City Reports, World-wide Press Comment, Company Information, Technical and Scientific Research given capital letters? Caps should be reserved for proper names or titles. This isn't Germany.
6   It is pointless to say 'and much more besides'. If there's more, say what the more is, or cut the phrase out altogether.
7   The release gives a contact name and number, and quite rightly says 'more/2' when it reaches the end of a page, but there's no indication that the story has ended. It's important to state clearly that the material is finished by writing 'end' or 'ends'.

To quote our Fleet Street editor: 'This is over-hyped waffle. Why don't they say what they mean instead of using tenth-rate ad jargon?'

Critique

1   Oh dear! What are they writing about – an afternoon at Henley or the marketing of a product? This isn't Jennifer's Diary in *Harpers and Queen*. No editor is interested in the description of a press launch, but in what the launch is about: the camera should have been mentioned right up-front, the high-falutin'

Press release 2

SNAPVISION LAUNCHES NEW CAMERA

[1] **Snapvision Europe feels privileged to be able to launch several brand new cameras onto the European market at an evening occasion at the Embassy of the United States of America in London. Harry Schneiderman, Vice-President of New Jersey based Snapvision Products Inc., welcomed several senior Ministers from the US Embassy Export Development Office, major UK and European customers and members of the press.**

The occasion heralded the introduction of the new Snap-Snap 35mm camera with its 2×Telewide option, and the new In-View 35 compact camera. All cameras are intended for the amateur photographic market where consumers have become accustomed to a simple point-and-shoot camera, producing consistent quality prints.

Comments Peter Jarvis, Managing Director of Coventry-based Snapvision Europe:
[2]
[3] **'These new cameras reflect our philosophy to provide modern, technologically advanced cameras at a low cost. They feature new styling and graphics, new attractive packaging, and most important to both merchandising and buyers and consumers alike, new pricing.'**

[4] **'We are dedicated to improving the product line and increasing the value of our Snapvision brands.'**

–End–

Media inquiries: Annette Blue   567 1100
Sales inquiries: Heather Jenns   567 1122

Surviving the Media Jungle

knees-up totally ignored. (What's an 'evening occasion' anyway?) The sentences are too long, with insufficient punctuation. You should break-up long units of type: dashes, colons and commas are editorial assets. And *any* journalist who reads words like 'Snapvision Europe feels privileged to be able to launch' goes into Hack's AWS (Automatic Wince Syndrome).

2 'These new cameras reflect our philosophy to provide'. 'Firstly, the grammar's wrong: it's 'our philosophy *in providing*', and anyway – *who cares* about their company philosophy!

3 The cost and low pricing are mentioned, but *what is it*? Surely low pricing is fundamental to the whole campaign, and surely they should mention the retail outlets that stock the cameras? It's like giving someone a box of half-eaten chocolates.

4 Quotes from managing directors and chief executives add a human touch to a release, and are usually a good idea, but not when they are cliché-ridden, yawn-inspiring gobbets of boredom like 'we are dedicated to improving our product line and increasing the value of our Snapvision brands'.

5 A release like this will rarely be of use to a features desk, unless it is doing a special feature on photography or unless the PRO can sell it in either in combination with a competition or other promotion, linked to a specific event such as the holiday season. There is no angle to tantalise a journalist in this story. Moral: unless you create one, keep mum.

Quote from our Fleet Street editor: 'This is pretentious tosh. The material is over-written to an absurd degree, and if they are promoting a low-cost camera, why don't they mention the damn price?'

If both these releases are a disgrace to publicity-seeking companies, the remedies are obvious, and easy to achieve. Writing good usable copy is within the grasp of most people. No one expects the business community to churn out press releases written with the elegance of Jane Austen, but if some basic rules of journalese are followed, most releases will at least hit their mark.

Rule 1

Write the releases on paper that identifies your company or product. It doesn't have to be over-expensive or elaborate, but some form of corporate identity or company logo makes your news stand out from the crowd, and journalists will recognise the letterhead. (This can work both ways: if you write lousy releases, they will be instantly binned unread.)

Rule 2

Identify the release as a release. Make sure that there is a release date clearly marked on the release. At the top of the page write 'Press release' or 'Press information' to identify your message. I dislike 'News release' – very few such releases actually contain real news. I'm in favour of the umbrella term often used in the USA – Communiqué

– but doubt whether this will catch on in a Britain notorious for its business parochialism.

Contact names, addresses and phone numbers are also essentials. They can either be at the beginning or end of the copy, but must be there. PR consultants should give both their name and number, and the client's, with the client's name predominating. A release date denotes topicality, and confirms embargoes. And *never* send old press releases, especially if you're announcing something new – you're defeating your own objectives.

Rule 3

Give each release a title – simple, tight and to the point, preferably identifying the story. If you feel confident about your style and wit, try a clever headline. The arguments about 'straight vs witty' headlines and style in releases rage as hot as ever. Some PR writers say wit doesn't work – the sub-editors doctor your copy anyway, so why do their job for them?

However, I'm all in favour of good, interesting writing if it achieves results. And so, since I have done the rounds and asked, is Fleet Street. Let's face it, if you were a journalist wading through 200 releases a day, what would catch your eye first – a 'label headline', with a straightforward, but flatly written story, or something that made you sit up, gasp, smile, frown, sneer, chuckle or groan?

Again common sense rules. High-tech, medical or financial releases will rarely, because of their very subject matter, lend themselves to wit and humour. But consumer releases often do. If there's a chance – take it. Even if the subs do rewrite your copy, at last you will have shown you have tried.

Rule 4

Use double spacing, or 1.5 spacing when writing, and wide margins either side of the text. Use A4 paper and write on one side of the page only.

These measures are important. Double spacing and margins not only look better, they also enable the subs to rewrite or alter the piece, and set down their printing instructions. Most singly spaced releases get dumped without being read. Using A4 paper is standard practice, and writing on one side of the paper assures a professional air.

Rule 5

Remember the 5 Ws. Answer the basic journalism questions – Who? What? Why? Where? and When? (and How?, if appropriate) – in the first paragraph. The introduction is the most important part of the release, for *if the jounalist only reads or prints that first para, it should stand up on its own*. For example, 'Snapvision Cameras is launching two new cameras on to the market this month: the Snap-Snap 35mm, and the In-View 35 compact'.

You have summarised the story clearly and concisely.

Surviving the Media Jungle

Everything else – the market the cameras are aimed at, Snapvision's reputation as a company, the quote from the managing director – follows in subsequent paragraphs. It's flesh on the bones.

Rule 6

Ensure releases follow a logical sequence. When you're talking, your sentences have a beginning, a middle and an end. So should releases. Plan the flow of content in your mind, or write down the features, benefits and facts about your company or product – what makes it special, attractive, useful, how much it costs, where to get it and so on. For example, the PRO for Snapvision could write this about the new camera ranges:

> Launched summer 1991.
> New range of compact small cameras for general consumer use. Auto-focusing, telewide options, point-to-shoot, other features.
> Competitively priced: only £12.99 and £15.99 respectively.
> Quote from MD about consumers wanting multi-function cameras, modestly priced: Snapvision fills this demand.
> Snapvision New Jersey, parent company, founded in 1923, most profitable US camera company. Profits up 25% last year.
> Mention retail outlets.

That's all you need to say. Each one of these headings

can then be expanded into a short paragraph. A perfectly usable release ensues.

Rule 7

Make each para concise and to the point: 40–50 words maximum. Similarly try and keep most releases to one page of A4 only.

The golden rule is keep it short. Busy newsrooms haven't time to wade through tons of copy. If you feel you are writing and writing and haven't reached the point, you may have got more than one story. Perhaps you should be writing *two* releases on slightly different angles instead of one.

For a technical release, in which you have a great deal of information to impart – e.g. 'Shutter fixed at 1/125 second. Flash: built in electronic 1/100 sec. Lens: three element, colour corrected, 38mm f:5.6: focus free – write separate background sheets listing the relevant details and attach them to the press release or press pack. Write on the bottom of the press release 'For further details, see accompanying sheets'. Journalists can then go straight to the relevant background sheets.

Don't be tempted to write your own sub-headings on the release; it may seem professional to you, but subs will have their own ideas. All that need concern you is the providing of bright, fresh copy.

Rule 8

If you haven't finished say so; if you have, confirm it. If you haven't managed to get your release on to one side of A4, then write 'more follows' or 'cont./2' at the end of the page. When you have finished, write 'End' or 'Ends'. It's good practice to do this because if your first sheet becomes detached from the second, at least a journalist knows there is more to look for; again, 'ends' confirms there is nothing more to say.

Rule 9

Don't embargo unless you absolutely have to. Businessmen and many PROs love embargoes: it looks so important writing the words 'EMBARGOED UNTIL 25 JUNE' in bold red type on a release. But most embargoes are pointless. Think again. When you are asking a journalist to embargo a story, you are asking him not to use the very tools of his trade – copy. Accessibility and usability are two key words in press relations: make life as easy for the press as possible.

There are occasions when embargoes are necessary, e.g. when announcing royal visits, or, in the financial world, when releasing annual results or other highly sensitive information that needs to be tightly controlled. But unless you are dealing with this sort of confidential story, try and avoid embargoes; they simply pile more paper into a journalist's already crowded in-tray.

Rule 10

Quotes add colour and act as time-savers. Providing

they are not simply a string of clichés praising the company to the skies, quotes from managing directors, staff and other concerned individuals bring a release to life with a humanising touch. They also help the press: quotes can be lifted out and inserted into press copy directly, if the journalist doesn't have the time to conduct a one-to-one interview or take the story further.

Style

Now that you have mustered the correct technical procedure of release writing, there's a little thing called style to worry about. I look on style as a subtle blend of flair and forward planning.

It is also an ephemeral animal. The most important thing to remember about writing is to feel comfortable with what you're doing. It's rather like handling media interviews: being yourself is the best policy. Taut, factual copy is *de rigueur*, and most people can manage to write in this straightforward way. If you have enough belief in your own presentation and style to be able to inject alliteration, humour, wit – fine. Otherwise stick to what you know.

Here are six guidelines for good writing which make life easier for me:

- **Grab the reader's attention in the first paragraph**. An interesting release is like a good speech – you have an average of 30 seconds in which to lose or win your audience. So try a startling statement like 'With 30,000 acres of rainforest being destroyed

Surviving the Media Jungle

every second, the Worldwide Fund for Nature today launches an awareness campaign . . .' or 'Baldies rejoice: Insta-fix hair restorer guarantees total hair replacement within 14 days'. Think about the language you are using. A thesaurus can help create variety.

- **Remember the magic of 'you'.** If you address your release to the reader rather than the third person, you instantly create immediacy and closeness between the writer and the reader. (You may have noticed I've adopted this convention for this book.) 'Do *you* suffer from baldness? Insta-fix will make *your* hair grow back within two weeks.'

- **Never assume the reader knows what you mean.** Even if something seems very basic to you, it may be complete double-Dutch to the reader. We all wallow in our own jargon, so explain fully, and as David Bernstein of the Creative Business says: 'Never assume – it makes an ASS of U and ME'.

- **Murder your darlings.** This is a quotation from the well-loved philosopher and essayist, Sir Arthur Quiller-Couch. Q would always tell his students to be their own best editors, and vigorously discard any purple passages in their prose. Sometimes it's hard to do: if you have slaved lovingly over a sentence, it's torture to run a blue pencil through it. The point is, over-writing doesn't lend itself to publicity purposes and leads to over-kill. Often the common touch is best. Read through your copy with your marketing hat on, polish and rewrite. You're creating merchandise, not sentiment.

HOW TO WRITE A PRESS RELEASE

- **Check your grammar and punctuation**. Both releases given to me by our zealous features editor made fundamental errors in grammar. They could have done with shorter paras and better punctuation too. Nothing succeeds better than a full stop.

  For longer sentences the semi-colon is a worthwhile asset; and write with a dash — dashes break up sentences and create a subtle link from thought to thought — rather useful little devices.

  If you are using an unusual spelling, write 'Jon (correct) Smith said today'. This lets the journalist know you are not a twit. If you are writing a release and thinking of the journalist when you write it, putting yourself in his shoes, reading it with his eyes, you can't go wrong.

- **Familiarise yourself with the styles of others**. Good writing thrives on good reading. The more you see how others do it, the greater your own facility. You'll probably find your friends and colleagues (and even occasionally journalists themselves!) very useful touchstones. If you're not sure about your press releases, especially in the early stages, ask for a second opinion. Constructive criticism (as opposed to senseless nitpicking) will help you enormously.

  The *Financial Times* style book, which is given to every new journalist on joining the paper, also gives pointers to make your copy sharper and more consistent. They include:

  – Don't insert full stops after capital letter abbreviations, e.g. BBC, ICI, DTI, etc.

- Write numbers one to ten out in full, but 11 onwards in numerals (the exception being thousands of millions, which look ridiculous in numerals).
- Never underline a news release. It's an instruction to the printers to set in italic type.
- Never over-use capital letters. Select only proper nouns, place names, titles, etc.

Clumsy writing

Even the most experienced writer sometimes finds himself being caught out by clumsy, awkward phraseology. Beware redundancies: saying two or more words when one will do, as in 'difficult problem', 'true facts'. If something's a problem, it's going to be difficult; if something is factual, it must also be true.

Such laboured phrases as 'with regard to' (concerning), 'at this moment in time' (now), and 'during the course of' (during) should also be avoided. The trick is to reread your copy, polish it and try and cut the wordage down. Tight editing is a hallmark of British journalism and should be adhered to.

Another trap which is very easy to fall into is to swamp your copy with clichés. Some are obvious, and the media are guilty of them as well – blondes are always 'bombshells' in the tabloids; Premium Bond or Pools wins of £100,000 or more are invariably 'staggering'; and even in the broadsheets, union unrest creates 'winters/summers of discontent' as the CBI 'fights union solidarity and industrial muscle', while trying to 'create an environment for meaningful discussions'.

HOW TO WRITE A PRESS RELEASE

The business world creates its own clichés. Computer-speak jargon accounts for a good deal: 'we need to create synergy, and a strong interface between customers and management'. So it goes on. Next time you find yourself writing about your company's 'dynamic new initiative' – take heart, take stock, but take care.

Try these exercises for size. What's wrong with the following paragraphs, and how can they be put right?

1. The Department of Maritime Studies at Bruddiford Technical College have recently acquired a Spearing Gyroscope Astral-Maritime Navigation Plotter with two 26" trimmer screens and adjustable crobble-switch, which will pre-set longitude to 54 adjustments within 15 seconds, and can be used in a temperature range of −55°C to +40°C.

2. Mr Cornelius Trubshawe, Director of Loamshire Institute of Psychiatry, and his Assistant Director Dr Ignatius Postlethwaite, have both been selected by the Department of Health to take part in the enquiry, chaired by Sir Joseph Axman, former Director-General of the British Society for the Protection of Fallen Women, into Psychiatric Research and Development Programmes in England and Wales.

3. At a meeting between officers of the Students Union of Langton College and the College's Joint Trades' Union Committee which represents almost 300 staff and which faces the biggest crisis in its history – the possible loss of 200 jobs over three years as a consequence of a £450,000 cut over that period – it was resolved to conduct a vigorous protest campaign to

alert the local community to the damage cuts of this magnitude will inflict on further education in the area.

Targeting

It's a mistake to think that one release will do as a blanket mail-out for all media outlets. I'm all in favour of writing two or three releases on the same subject, specially targeted and specifically written. Not enough companies and PROs do this.

When I suggest this in my lectures, many executives reel in horror and say they don't have the time. I would argue that such definite targeting is worth the investment, as it will yield quantifiable results.

Most press releases can be targeted as follows:

- One to the trade (factual, technical, can use jargon, as they will understand what you mean).

- One to broadsheets and quality magazines/ programmes (factual, formal, succinct).

- One to tabloids, popular magazines/programmes and lightweight consumer magazines and programmes (chatty, informal, full of human interest).

As an exercise, try and rewrite the Retrieve release (p. 82) in three different ways, and you'll find that the whole process of targeting suddenly comes to life. It may take time to get the technique right, but it's worth it.

Photographs

If you can send a pic with a release, do so. The whys and wherefores of press photography are explored more fully in Chapter 6.

Faxes

One last thing: with the growth of electronic mail, it is tempting to think that the old-fashioned way of sending a press release by post has had its day, and that tomorrow's releases will be transmitted by facsimile machine alone. Some public relations companies are already adopting the horrible method of regularly sending out releases via Fax. I think this is very unwise; junk faxes are as irritating as junk mail, and the danger that news editors will simply dump the day's pile of faxes into the bin unread is not unreasonable.

Faxes take time to print out, and a PR release could well clog up space needed for an urgent news communiqué. If this continues, there may even come a time when facsimile machines have numbers known only to editorial staff, and kept for editorial use only, rather like a private password.

If PR executives are responsible for this through the mailing of indiscriminate faxes, it will be a shame. Let's face it: you have to pay not only for the faxes you send out, but for the faxes you receive, so undoubtedly editorial staff will handle faxes with care.

Only send a release via Fax if the release is particularly urgent or newsworthy. Crisis, yes, product launch, no. Use the Big Deal test for fax transmission of press releases.

6

Watch the birdie

The first rule of PR photography is to remember that the best PR pictures are the ones taken by newspaper photographers themselves. It's one of the reasons why the names of magazine or newspaper picture editors should be as familiar to the publicity-seeking executive as the names of business or feature editors. Well-organised photo-calls, with a product which is not over-plugged and which offers good photo opportunities, are unbeatable in the eyes of the press.

High on the hit-list of news and picture editors are boring, dull, uninteresting photographs, many of them PR inspired, which land willy-nilly across their desks on a busy morning. Top of the range of pet hates include:

- Photographs of worthy individuals holding giant cheques donated by some worthy company for some worthy cause.

- Photographs of local branch managers of little-known companies who have just been appointed to their new position.

- Photographs of company directors of little-known companies who have just been appointed to their new position.

Surviving the Media Jungle

- Photographs of lesser celebrities endorsing the launch of the latest consumer gadget.

- Photographs of the latest consumer gadget, with no caption and no product information.

- Girls (often in swimsuits) sitting on/handling/ smiling at the latest consumer gadget.

- Public relations practitioners who phone up asking if the editor has used any of the above.

This is a pity, because, properly used, photography is a key communications tool, and the old adage 'a pic is worth one thousand words' still holds good. Try and visualise photo opportunities in your mind when you are writing a release or planning a campaign. Nothing is more arresting, or illustrates a point better, than an eye-catching visual. But like all aspects of media relations, photography needs to be carefully handled to succeed. Pictures for pictures' sake are expensive time-wasters.

If you are not organising a photo-call but overseeing the shoot yourself, the first thing to ask yourself is what do you want the picture for? Is it a product shot intended for a trade magazine? Will it be marketed to consumers, or is the photograph the visual element of a news story? The approach will be different in each case, *and press photography should be tailored just as a press release is tailored*.

That means understanding your markets, and making sure your photographer does too. If the picture is intended for a national newspaper, why not phone up the picture desk and ask what sort of pictures would be appropriate?

WATCH THE BIRDIE

Local dignitary presents local businessman with award for raising money for charity.

   I'm sure it's all in a good cause – and if you look very carefully you will see that the gentleman in question is wearing a Cancer Relief badge – but it's such a yawn. The picture tells us nothing. The smiles are a trifle fixed – and what is the local dignitary actually presenting? For all we know, it could be a gold watch on his retirement (*Orpington News Shopper*).

Surviving the Media Jungle

Scanvision launch new camera.

   Oh dear! How predictable – the very kind of PR picture editors would like us to avoid. Just snap a pretty girl with a camera, and cross your fingers. It's not enough – for a start, she's not even focusing the thing properly, and if the cafetière and *Le Monde* (at foot) are trying to create a continental atmosphere, it's very laboured.

Choosing your photographer

Much PR photography is poor quality, but it needn't be if you have chosen the right men for the job. That means no do-it-yourself. Unless you have the talents of a David Bailey, I would strongly recommend that you seek a professional photographer.

There are many directories which can help you choose, and you will find a list in Appendix 1. The Institute of Professional Photography produces an annual register listing members, which you can buy, and you can also contact the National Union of Journalists photographers' branch. Directories such as *PNA* and *Editors*, and the PR Bible *Hollis*, also list such reputable photo agencies as Bill Hennessy Associates and other Fleet Street agencies who can produce commercial work.

You will find that over the years you build up a portfolio of photographers who each specialise in different jobs. This is particularly so in the PR industry, where you work across a variety of accounts and consistently need a fresh look at the same subject. It's a mistake to think that a photographer can do everything: professionals who concentrate on food and drink are very unlikely to be experts on industrial photography, for example.

When selecting a photographer, don't choose on spec. Make sure you see examples of work he has done, to give you an idea of his range and content. You may even care to visit his studio and chat to him on the premises. It's actually quite advisable. You can discover a lot about people by observing their work environment. If the studios look dingy and disorganised, and the phone is always ringing with complaining clients, it's best to look elsewhere.

Surviving the Media Jungle

Picture to commemorate Estonia's first fax link with the West, engineered by British Telecom International.

Yes, this is for real – but it took me 5 minutes to stop laughing when I first saw it. Just in case we missed the point that we were dealing with the Eastern bloc, there's a bust of Lenin, a picture of Gorbachev, a copy of Pravda (not in Cyrillic script, incidentally) and my Russian spies tell me that the periodical next to it is the equivalent of *Farmers' Weekly*. Somewhere in the corner, you can just make out 'British Telecom Gateway to the . . .'

This is a picture where the PRO was trying too hard. Detail is all very well, but there's far too much of everything. (And when did you last see an Estonian who looked like Bertie Wooster?)

Brief your photographer properly. He has the technical expertise of course, but you know what you need. Your photographic needs will be different if you want a product shot for a newspaper or an illustration for an in-house magazine.

Write out the brief and give him a copy – specifying all details if possible. If the shoot is on location, it's a good idea for you and the photographer to visit the place beforehand, so that angles can be planned effectively. Studio work is less demanding, but in all cases you should be there on the day of the shoot. There may be last-minute changes to the brief that need to be discussed, and while you should not interfere if everything is going well, you should speak up and make your presence felt if you are unhappy at the way he is tackling the job.

What to take

Try and obtain a selection of shots, with different angles, setting varied moods and styles. If you're photographing a computer, the hardware by itself may be sufficient for a trade publication, but a predictable product shot like that will be quite unsatisfactory for a consumer publication or a newspaper.

Think story-line in each case, and target accordingly. You may well need life and animation in the shot – people, animals. Can you try an amusing approach to the picture? A photograph showing a toddler or a chihuahua operating the computer's terminals will be a lot easier to place, and a great deal more arresting, than a

Surviving the Media Jungle

lifeless shot of a screen. One trick of the trade is to show comparative sizes – the clothes shop High and Mighty, which caters for very large and very tall gentlemen, once pictured a man of 6'6" next to a man of 4'7" with a 52" chest! Other special effects can be achieved by the artful use of colour-mixing or superimposition.

In addition, there are newspaper variations. Just as the *Sun* wants a chatty release, it wants busy, breezy pictures too. The picture should reflect the style of the publication to which it will be sent.

A common fault for many photographs that use company personnel is for the subjects to end up looking stiff and unnatural, or turn up in ridiculously formal wear, quite unsuitable for a photo-session. It's up to you to tell them what to wear beforehand, and up to the photographer to try to make them feel at ease. Often they will relax if they are pictured at work, doing what they know and understand. If the end results are quite impossible, it may be you will have to use professional models, but normally they should be a last resort for industrial-type photography – they just don't look believable.

Of course it is a good idea to build up a portfolio of models and model agencies for specialised work such as hair and beauty products, and models should be chosen as you would choose a photographer, according to their experience and their suitability for the job. There are many agencies listed in directories, and your photographer should prove a mine of information, and may well have built up a good working relationship with several agencies.

Formats

Even in these days of full colour printing in newspapers most editors still normally require black and white – 8" × 6" or 10" × 8" glossy prints – and it goes without saying that these should be well composed and well focused. (That's why you brought in the professionals!) Colour magazines normally require 35mm colour transparencies and stills for television purposes are normally 10" × 8" matt colour.

You should know these requirements before shooting, and if you need to check with individual publications to make sure, there's no harm in asking. Tell your photographer what they want – different printing processes determine what lighting is used, and how much detail can be included.

I'm a great believer in photographers bringing along a selection of equipment, so that you can shoot both colour and black and white at the same time. This way you can satisfy several markets at once. Photography is after all an expensive business, and if you can capitalise on your session, so much the better!

Press release distribution agencies are often used to send out pictures. But blanket mail-out of pictures, like blanket mail-out of press releases, is never a good idea. A selection of shots – perhaps two or three – to selected publications is a much better bet. Make sure you mail photographs in boarded envelopes, clearly marked PHOTOGRAPHS: DO NOT BEND. Nothing is worse than unwrapping creased, tatty pictures. Make sure they get there on time: missing deadlines is always suicidal, but never more so when you are sending out a picture for a news story. Even though the press will normally send

Surviving the Media Jungle

their staff photographers to cover these events, if for one reason or another they are relying on you, don't mail the shot first class. Bike it or courier it instead!

Picture to commemorate National Low Drink Week, aimed at persuading young people to drink low-alcohol and non-alcoholic beverages. It almost works and it is a very good pic. The kids are enjoying themselves, and you can see they're getting into the spirit of the evening (quite literally). Lots of L.A. booze and orange juice prominently on display. Pity the badges don't show up better though (*Orpington News Shopper*).

Captions

Photographs which arrive without captions are a newsroom bugbear. Pictures with no contact name, phone number or address, and sent completely out of context, are a total waste of editorial time. When you think about it, it's not only careless, but downright stupid to send out unattributed information – especially as captions are simply common sense.

At its most simple form, a caption is a gummed label, stuck to the back of a photograph, with a title and a short summary of the action: 'Holsten Pils Point-to-Point. March 18 1991. The winner of the Bedfordshire Trophy. From L to R: Mrs Anna Huntingdon-Smythe presenting the Trophy to Captain Lancelot Wills.' This kind of caption is perfect for short, pithy pieces, probably intended for local news outlets or special interest/trade journals.

Longer, more detailed photo-stories require longer, more detailed captions. The caption in this case is no different to a press release, written with all the succinctness of a news story, and enclosing details of the picture. But don't swamp the caption with words: if it's a picture story, the picture should really do most of the talking.

In this instance the release is typed on A4 paper, either gummed or sellotaped to the back of the photograph, and folded to fit the picture. There are drawbacks to both methods: gum can crinkle the photograph when it dries, and sellotape can be torn away. Perhaps, on points, sellotape is best.

It's inadvisable for your photographer to stamp the back of the photographs with his own label for two reasons: firstly, you should be the main point of contact; secondly, if the photographer is not an NUJ member, editors might not use his pictures in times of industrial action. The sensitivities of the British press are manifold.

Copyright

Normally, copyright of any picture taken for PR purposes remains with the sender (you). This means that editors can use it freely without paying a reproduction fee. It is therefore unnecessary to state who owns the copyright on the back of the picture. Photographs hired from press agencies retain their own copyright.

Picture agencies/Photo-libraries

Sometimes you may need to consult photographic libraries or picture agencies to locate specific shots of archive, scientific or other material. Redferns, for example, is one of the UK's largest music picture libraries, with more than 3,000 pictures on stock; Planet Earth specialises in wildlife and environmental photographs. The Hulton Picture Library is probably the most famous, and has the largest selection. A fee is normally charged, and it is rare that footage of this kind is used for PR-style photography, though you may well require this kind of picture for newsletters, calendars or brochures.

You should also begin to build up a photo-library of your own, cataloguing each photographer and the work

WATCH THE BIRDIE

he has done for you, on individual topics and for individual clients. Have several copies of selected photographs always available – they include the 'stock shots' of key executives and product lines. This kind of photo-library is an invaluable reference source, for both your company and the press. It means you are never caught

Natural History Museum picture to publicise the Dinosaurs Live! Exhibition.
   I don't need to say anything about this picture. It's wonderful. It's alive, brimming with vitality, a perfect PR shot. It made the covers of several national newspapers, and deservedly so. And I think *T. Rex* is rather cute. (*Natural History Museum*)

Surviving the Media Jungle

out. If a journalist requests a stock shot, there will always be one in-house.

Unfortunately too many libraries contain out-of-date product and personality shots, or aren't able to come up with the goods. This is both sloppy and unprofessional, and doesn't help build contacts with the press, or indeed within your own organisation.

Good pictures are an asset, and if you develop an eye for a picture, there will be many opportunities available to create newsworthy and interesting feature material. But it's not a magic trick – anyone can do it. Look at the newspapers and see the stories that make the headlines. In 90 per cent of cases you will see that it's very simple: a well-shot photo, allied to one or more of the angles we discussed in Chapter 4, makes the news every time.

7

Bring on the gin and tonic

Ask what the words 'press publicity' mean to the average company director, and he will probably answer gleefully: 'press conferences'. Company directors love press conferences. They are an opportunity for executives to swan around importantly, meeting the press and pompously holding forth. The actual reason for such an event is often never questioned. Like Everest, MDs want press conferences organised because they are there.

In fact press conferences are the bane of a journalist's life. They are invited to several hundred every week, and for every worthwhile, newsworthy event, such as the opening of the Channel Tunnel, definitely listed in their diary under YES!, there are twenty or thirty yawn-makers, such as the launch of a repackaged me-too product with no intrinsic interest except to the trade. These will be instantly binned.

Just as journalists number badly written press releases among their pet hates, so time-wasting, boring press conferences come high on their dart-board. It's a mistake to think that journalists will drop everything for a free lunch and endless rounds of Scotch. As one PR wag put it, 'the importance of a press conference story is inversely proportional to the amount of booze dispensed'. In

Surviving the Media Jungle

other words, the weaker the story, the stronger the spirits. But most journalists are professionals first and bon viveurs later. That means coming back with a story, not a hangover.

When the idea of a press conference is mooted, the first thing to ask yourself is: 'Do I really need it?' These events can be very expensive, and to succeed they must be well-run. Could the event be best organised and publicised by other means? Would a one-to-one interview with your company's MD or marketing manager be sufficient? Or a press release accompanied by a well-composed photograph? Would a facility visit to your factory, showing-and-telling the journalists on the premises, be a more satisfactory way of disseminating information?

In inviting journalists to a press conference you are asking them to give up half their day to your company, time they could use writing or researching other stories. Make sure the conference is worth their while, or you will find that next time you organise a media event they will be unlikely to turn up. A badly run and unnecessary press conference is one of the quickest ways to lose friends among the press. Once lost, it's difficult to win them back.

Of course it's important to foster good press liaison, and essential to cultivate a close working relationship with the press. Meetings between company representatives and the media ensure clear communications. Press events are just one of the means to this end, and there are several guidelines to their successful organisation. The first point to remember is that the press conference is just one of several ways to initiate face-to-face contact with the press. The other ways are:

- One-to-one interviews.
- Press briefings.
- Facility visits.
- Photo-calls.
- Formal or news conferences.

Each has its use and relevant function within the media relations campaign. Naturally, as with all media contact, selectivity is important. You need to choose the right publications and media outlets for each event.

One-to-one interviews

Let's say a new managing director has been appointed to a large manufacturing company. He is the first new MD in 25 years, and likely to initiate a 'new broom sweeps clean' approach to corporate matters.

You could hold a press conference to introduce him to the press – the company is after all a multi-national, with an excellent reputation – but press conferences are often stilted and highly organised events, not designed to foster close relations with the media. Your new MD would probably benefit more by meeting four or five journalists on a one-to-one basis. The publications and newspapers you choose should be properly targeted and relevant – perhaps a mixture of national, local and trade – and it's advisable that several story angles are discussed and approved with your MD in advance, so that the journalists' copy is varied, and reflects the many faces of the company and the MD's role within the organisation.

In Michael Frayn's play *Clouds* two reporters from two

Surviving the Media Jungle

rival colour magazines find they are after the same 'exclusive' story on the same day. The PRO frantically juggles their schedules so that each comes away happy with a different news-splash. The ensuing chaos makes for an amusing play – but *you* needn't be caught out. One-to-one interviews are not 'exclusives', and they don't have to be. In any case 'exclusives' are nearly always one paper's excuse for tomorrow's news everywhere else; news travels and exclusives are rarely exclusives for long. There are times when it's good business practice to offer an exclusive to the press – say you want to really build up a sound relationship with one particular paper – but never over-use exclusives.

Before the journalists arrive, make a careful study of their publications. What is the style like? Are they aggressive or confrontational? Do they report in more general terms? Is the journalist a specialist reporter on your industry? What sort of questions are likely to be asked? Only when you have addressed yourself to these questions, and briefed your MD accordingly, should he be let loose!

Should you, as PRO, be present at the interview? This all depends on your MD's confidence and experience. A seasoned interviewee requires little back-up from public relations except a good background knowledge of the journalists concerned. Less professional interviewees may need support and guidance, and a discreet presence could be valuable, to help steer the interview along the correct path. But the emphasis is on the word 'discreet'. Nothing irritates a reporter more than a pushy PRO who gets in the way. Besides – who's being interviewed, the PRO or the MD? Again it's best to use common sense.

Journalists should be given as much background

material as they need – annual reports, corporate brochures, press releases on individual company products, photographs, biographies of key personnel. This means maintaining an up to date press library.

Journalists are often invited to stay for lunch after the interview. Their schedule will dictate whether they will or not. If they do, slap-up lunches or exotic drinks are not necessary or appropriate. A simple lunch either at the company executive dining-room (if the fare is edible) or a nearby restaurant is quite sufficient. The interview could even be conducted informally over lunch – except that it's often tricky for journalists to take notes with napkins tucked under the chin!

One-to-one interviews offer unmatched opportunities for executives and the media to meet on equal terms. Each gets to know more about the other's activities and objectives, and when they are properly handled, that can only build equity and improved relations.

Press briefings

These are similar to one-to-ones, except that (a) up to ten journalists from similar media areas are invited and (b) more than one representative of the company can be present. Press briefings, if you like, are mini press conferences, but news is imparted to the right sources on a more intimate footing. The briefings allow for in-depth questioning and explanation, and targeting is assured.

One of the most comprehensive briefings I have seen was for a leading chemical company. Twelve months earlier, the firm had introduced on to the market a new plastic, which had multi-faceted industrial applications. When the product was first announced, there had been a major press conference which had been well attended and well reported. As a follow-up a year later the company held a press briefing in London, to show selected journalists just how European industry had taken advantage of the product.

Four representatives of senior management from France, Germany, Switzerland and Italy brought samples, slides and literature, which they showed to ten journalists, each of whom wrote for different trade magazines, including magazines dealing with plastics. Questions were answered at length, and covered a wide variety of areas. Each journalist was given a sample of the product in its untreated state to take away, and full background notes on its industrial usage. A copy of the product video was also available on request.

The briefing was held in the boardroom of an elegant London club, and questions were continued informally in the club dining-room. Company executives were represented at each of the press tables. It was a briefing aimed at the trade, but the national press (which reads trade publications for background use) followed the story up; a column duly appeared, giving an update on the product's European industrial success, in the Innovations page of the *Sunday Times*.

Facility visits

As the name implies, facility visits allow the press on to your premises or into your factory, but they could also

BRING ON THE GIN AND TONIC

include visiting a newly opened airport terminal, jumping on board an ocean liner, or a trip to premises overseas. These are good times to impart information, but such visits have to be handled with care.

Firstly, decide what kind of visit it is. Will you be using the journalists' arrival as a news-peg to hang an important official announcement on, or are you treating the visit as an opportunity to build good relations and provide background material?

If the visit is one for background purposes, make sure everyone – and that means workers as well as management – knows the journalists are coming. One of the most embarrassing trips I ever made as a journalist was to a drinks company where no one had informed personnel that I was visiting that day. Not only were few people prepared to talk to me, but I was unable to watch certain processes I had specifically requested to see. There's no point allowing a facility visit if you're not prepared or briefed enough to show journalists the facilities!

This doesn't mean the press should wander around indiscriminately. Relevant personnel should be on hand to guide them and answer questions. If there are areas out of bounds, such as top-secret research and development areas, these should be pointed out to the journalists right at the start, to pre-empt any awkward moments later on.

If possible, try and find out each journalist's special interests in advance, so you can 'slot them in' with relevant personnel when they arrive. This gives them the story-angle they're looking for, and makes you look bright eyed and on the ball.

Remember, facility visits require expense and organisation. You have to look after the press. They have not

Surviving the Media Jungle

come for a fun day at the seaside, and they are your guests during the whole of their stay. It's likely that you will have to arrange for the journalists to be collected and brought to your premises, especially if your factory or offices are outside London, and return them that evening. Some may need to be accommodated overnight.

They will appreciate a timetable of events, starting from the moment they are picked up at their house or railway station, through to the moment they are deposited outside their front door. From your point of view a clear programme will help you run events to a controlled and defined schedule. Leave ample time for the factory tour, a possible presentation by management, viewing of the factory exhibition/museum/shop area, conversations and interviews with personnel and management, refreshments, etc. Try and rehearse and time the event with members of your team, and make sure everyone knows the full extent of their on-the-day responsibilities. You cannot be over-rehearsed. The more you plan in advance, the less of a worry the visit will be.

When it comes to refreshments, a buffet lunch on the premises is perfectly acceptable at the factory canteen. The press have come for a story not a gourmet feast. However, if your canteen suffers in the Egon Ronay stakes, and offers typically stodgy and indigestion-inducing fare, outside caterers can be brought in. Of course there's always the local restaurant or hotel if your own premises are simply not suitable. Check the dietary requirements of your guests in advance: requests for vegetarian, kosher or other special diets should be respected.

The same specifications apply if you have tied the

press visit to coincide with a news story, but here you must remember that speed is of the essence. The press may need facilities to relay the story back to their news desks. You will probably have to organise a press room with sufficient typewriters, word processors, telephones, fax or telex machines for the job. A darkroom facility may also be required. If you have invited radio and television, special arrangements may have to be made for them to film or record their interviews in advance. We'll come to radio and TV in Chapter 8.

Facility visits offer unequalled opportunities for the media to find out about your business. But again, don't invite them if you have nothing of any great import to say. You must be able to demonstrate, illustrate, elucidate, and leave the journalist feeling that the trip has provided valuable copy.

Photo-calls

Supposing you are a manufacturer of glamorous ski wear, aimed at the Klosters set. It's late in November, and Britain is preparing for a cold and frosty winter. You have already arranged glossy photo-sessions with *Vogue* magazine and *Harpers* on a one-to-one basis – since you've done your homework, all this was done in June, and you're looking forward to the January issues. But you would like to reach the national up-market papers (*The Times, Daily Telegraph, Independent*), you promised the fashion editor of the *Mail* a run-down on après-ski, and wasn't there a rumour that *Woman's Weekly* was going to do an in-depth report on skiing?

Surviving the Media Jungle

A photo-call will probably be the right kind of press activity here. Invitations to the appropriate newspaper picture desks are issued, stating when, where, and in what way the photo-call will be held. For fashion editors this kind of information is sufficient: their specialist photographers will do the rest, and bring along the equipment they need.

But for cynical news desks, bear in mind that photo-calls offer just that – photo opportunities – so the setting and composition should be arresting. The invitation should hint at the fact that your event is not simply another pretty girl on a dry ski slope. You've got to 'grab them', and get them there. How you do this is one of the challenges you face in publicity work. One answer is to place the ski-wear-clad model in an unusual setting or engaged in the kind of activity you don't normally associate with skiing – for example, you might get a well-known TV weather man to give an impromptu weather forecast, 'Snow and sun, perfect for the piste', wearing the suit. If you join forces with a travel company which organises glossy skiing holidays, you may be able to share the story with them, so both of you benefit from the publicity.

Picture desks are always complaining that photo-calls are excuses for blatant advertising of the product, and that 90 per cent of pictures taken at such events can never be used by an 'objective press'. It will need all your ingenuity to come up with the right balance to satisfy all parties – but that's the challenge to your expertise.

Photo-calls are not elaborate affairs. You don't have to provide food and drink – coffee is optional – but if the event is held outside on a bitterly cold day, thermos flasks of hot tea and coffee in plastic mugs will be appreciated.

You should ensure that the photographers have enough space and light to be able to shoot, so look out for cramped conditions or dark shadowy corners, and be prepared to lay on extra lighting if necessary. Relevant background material, facts, figures, or anything of special newsworthiness about the product or event should also be supplied, so that the journalist can write his caption. Sometimes photo-calls can be organised alongside one-to-one interviews. For example, if the ski-suit is made of a particularly rare or interesting material, the designer can be on hand to answer questions.

When it comes to dealing with the national daily press, here's a tip: new technology means that picture desks have to make up their pages much earlier now – the first ones are done by noon. So from a picture desk point of view the best photocalls are held at 10.00 am on a Sunday morning, and the worst at 4.00 pm on a Friday.

Press conferences

Press conferences can be divided into two categories: the 'soft' or 'formal' conference, which is usually feature-based, or 'news'.

News conferences

As their name suggests, news conferences are prompted by an event such as a company takeover or a crisis, and need to be held at short notice. They don't have to be staged affairs: the press will come for the story, nothing else.

Surviving the Media Jungle

Invitation can be by telephone, fax, or telex, and the conference itself can be held at company HQ or a central hotel. Refreshments are kept to a minimum – tea or coffee – and there is no need for 'packaging': colourful press packs are unnecessary, a simple typed statement or copies of the speeches being enough.

A news conference rarely lasts long. The whole thing could be over well within the hour. One or two leading executives issue short, planned statements, and the floor is then opened up for questions; photographs may be taken, TV camera crews film, then the journalists leave.

Of course if the story is particularly hot, you may need to organise a press room, with enough telephone lines, fax/telex and typewriters to cope. TV and radio journalists may also wish to interview the managing director or other executives, so a quiet room should be available. Only you can decide if this is necessary, but it's best to plan for such contingencies in advance, so that you're perfectly prepared.

Press conferences proper

Right! You really, hand-on-your-heart-truly, need a 'presser' with all the trimmings. You know who you want to invite. But there are three essential questions that need answering: when are you going to hold the conference, where, and how will it be run?

Timing is crucial, and you will never be able to please all of the press all of the time. Press conference timing is inevitably a compromise. Obviously, as we have seen, the nature of the event dictates the time of year the conference will be held. But the day of the week is also important.

Monday is a fairly good day for dailies, as the beginning of the week is notoriously low in news, but other journalists are often busy and unable to attend. Wednesday is normally press day for journalists working on weeklies. Friday is often rushed and too near the end of the week. Mid-month is a bad time for monthly magazines, because that is when they make up their pages. So a *Tuesday or a Thursday in the first or last 10 days of the month* may be one solution to attract a cross-section of media.

Deadlines create their own constraints. If you want the story splashed across the evening papers, then remember that 12 noon is closing time. Normally, however, pressers run from 10.30 am or 11.30 am to lunchtime, with journalists staying on for refreshments if they can afford the time to do so.

Breakfast receptions have been increasing in popularity over the last few years, owing to American influence. It is worth thinking in terms of breakfast receptions, because (a) they are over by 10 am, which means the journalists can go back to their desks with little time wasted, and (b) the novelty factor is still strong enough to attract the press.

A few crusty old-timers still around prefer their morning lie-ins, but you should encounter little resistance to an 8.30 or 9.00 am press call. One of the beauties of breakfasts is that they can be as informal or unusual as you wish, and can often be linked to your product: if you were an importer of tropical fruits, the breakfast would create an excellent opportunity for serving a delicious fruit salad; a producer of filter coffee machines could have a range of different coffees brewing away on display, and so on.

You should be thinking of planning the conference at

least 2 or 3 months in advance. This not only gives you plenty of time to organise, and book your speakers and/or celebrities, but it also ensures you are not holding your conference on the day of a conflicting event. You can certainly avoid unnecessary clashes with such events as national exhibition openings or other press conferences. The *Financial Times* publishes a guide to weekly events, and such monthly publications as the *Exhibitions Bulletin* are also useful. *PR Week* has a comprehensive reference section, and, on payment of a fee, the Daily Telegraph Information Bureau can come up with a suitable list.

However, you can't plan for a crisis or a sudden news-story blowing up on the day. I well remember organising a telecommunications seminar, with more than thirty journalists turning up, only to find them sneaking out halfway through, with the speakers still on the podium: news had leaked that the actor Roger Moore was pulling out of the Andrew Lloyd Webber musical *Aspects of Love*, and the journalists were speedily migrating to Moore's hastily arranged press conference!

The *venue* is another important consideration. Budget will obviously dictate where the event will be held. Hotels and clubs are often firm favourites, and indeed if they are in the centre of London, this ensures that journalists who work in the EC4, EC2, W1 and SE1 areas can easily attend. Transport considerations such as bus, tube and taxi are essential, and even though it seems that Fleet Street has emigrated to Docklands, the consumer press at National Magazine House and IPC shouldn't be ignored!

But a venue with a difference will often create press interest, and maybe nudge the balance between 'Should

I go?' and 'Definitely on the list!' Originality is always the best policy if it fits in with your client's marketing strategy.

The venue could be a zoo or a cinema, a pleasure boat or a site of historic interest, a racing track or an Oxbridge college. Whatever venue you choose, it should fit in with your public relations plans, and enhance the image you are promoting.

The venue should also be able to cope with your technical and administrative requirements. Are there facilities for the playing of videos of audio-visual material? Is there enough power for TV cameras? Are there enough telephones? Will there be enough light for photographers? Ample parking? Is there enough room to exhibit your product to its full advantage? You should make a checklist of your requirements well in advance, and pass this list to the colleagues who are helping you organise the conference. You'll find a sample checklist at the end of the chapter (p. 142).

There are other considerations too. Do you need a platform and dais for speakers? How will you arrange the seating? Do you need a non-smoking area and a quiet room for radio or TV interviews? And just as importantly – does the venue have a good reputation for catering? Will their chef suffice, or will you have to organise outside caterers? Again, budget will be a criterion here: a finger buffet is obviously less expensive per head than a four-course meal.

Once you have decided where and when the conference will be held, it's time to check the invitation list. You will probably invite the press most likely to cover the event, plus a mixture of freelancers, company guests and selected personnel. A well-organised press office will

Surviving the Media Jungle

have an up-to-date media list to hand, and directories such as *Editors* and *PNA* will help flesh out the gaps.

Try and be as wide-ranging as you can. Some time ago Amstrad deliberately left off the tabloid journalists from its press conference list, thinking that the *Sun*, *Mirror* and *Star* would be uninterested in computing. The company received angry phone calls from the tabloid journalists, complaining that they had been ignored! This kind of thing doesn't foster good press relations, so if you're unsure whether a journalist would be interested in your products, the sensible thing is to phone up and ask.

The nature of the event also dictates the form of the invitation. For a formal press conference a personal letter to selected journalists can often be enough, but there's still a lot to be said for printed invitation cards. Such cards can be highly stylised and conventional, outrageously arty, or funny in shape or content, depending on the nature of the product or service you are promoting.

If the event is worth spending money on, then it's worth the investment of a special card, with your company logo, and the journalist's name written by hand. This kind of personalised treatment never fails to get a good response; even if the journalist can't attend, an invitation of this sort dictates an answer out of courtesy.

The invitation should of course give details of the event, date, time, place, what kind of refreshments will be served, and a contact name and phone number for correspondence. You should also enclose a map of how to get there if the venue is difficult to find, or if the event is being held outside London and the press are making their own transport arrangements. A timetable of events

BRING ON THE GIN AND TONIC

will also be useful, for journalists will often only be able to come for part of the conference.

Bearing in mind that journalists receive several hundred invitations every week, it's a good idea to include a 'grabber' in the invitation – something that will make the press sit up and take notice. This could be a press release accompanying the invitation hinting that a Very Important Story will break on the day of the conference, or a small gift/item relating specifically to the conference itself.

Successful 'grabbers' have included a cork with the journalist's name written on it, inserted in an invitation to an English wine tasting, and a bottle of English Chablis on presentation of the cork; a garden fork and trowel at the opening of an exclusive garden centre; and a health questionnaire, charting personal fitness, alongside an invitation to the launch of a slimming margarine. The journalists' charts were individually analysed by fitness experts at the launch.

The trick is to make the grabbers intriguing and of definite interest to the journalists concerned, but they musn't be cute or cloying. Remember the comments of the *Daily Express* writer regarding pop-up perfumed flowers!

The press should be invited 5 or 6 weeks before the conference, and that will give you time enough to draw up acceptance and refusal lists. Since journalists are busy – but also notoriously lazy – a prepaid or stamped reply card included with the invitations should give a fairly accurate indication as to correct numbers. Invitations should always be sent out well in advance, because if three weeks before the conference you discover that attendance is looking pitifully thin, you still have time to

Surviving the Media Jungle

do a second mail-shot, targeting new or different media outlets.

Prepaid reply cards are useful, but no substitute for personal contact. Even if they've said yes, telephone the press the day before. This isn't a foolproof way of gauging numbers, however.

For a start, most journalists say they get irritated with this kind of 'hounding', and will refuse to give an answer. There's no easy way out: you can only be as polite as possible when you ring around, apologising for bothering them, but state your case. They have a job to do, and you've got yours.

What you mustn't do is put the press under undue pressure. Phil Harding of *Today* complains bitterly of public relations practitioners who get past his secretary by saying that their call is 'personal and private', only to ask him if *Today* will be attending a press conference. Since Harding has a policy of always accepting personal calls, he considers this a very sneaky way of worming in to his office. It is clearly not in the interest of good press relations for this kind of underhand behaviour to take place, and PROs should know better.

They should also know that very few journalists are going to give an outright 'no' when asked if they're coming to a presser. They will come if it's of genuine interest, or it's a low news day; they won't if they have a better news story to chase – so they figure that it's better to hedge their bets. This kind of shilly-shallying drives PROs into a frenzy, because they are desperate to tell their client they are expecting a good turn-out. But that's the nature of news. You can never predict attendance.

Even if you have a good number of acceptances, a good rule of thumb is to assume that for every fifty people who have agreed to attend, thirty will actually show up. There are many reasons for this – there may be a sudden urgent story to cover, there may be a change of heart. Whatever the reason, a few favourite freelancers who can be called on at the last minute are often a good stopgap. Another way to avoid last-minute embarrassment is to put out chairs for only half the number you expect. You can always add extra chairs later, and it looks better if it appears you have had a rush on the door.

Now you have chosen the venue, agreed on the catering and invited the guests, you must formulate the programme. How is the day going to be run? How will you demonstrate the product effectively? Will you have an audio-visual presentation? How many speakers will participate? A slickly orchestrated conference is essential. You cannot be over-prepared. Timing and rehearsal are crucial.

Nothing is more boring to journalists than a sit-down 'do', where they are handed out a press pack and expected to sit through a tedious 30 minutes of speeches, followed by a 30-minute corporate video or a/v which gushes over the virtues of the company concerned. There's nothing wrong with showing your glossy video to the press, but videos and audio-visual presentations are a bit of a yawn nowadays – everybody's showing them, and they do tend to go on and on. A 5-minute video clip, or selected slides which concentrate on highlights of a company's activities, is preferable.

The same rules apply to speeches. Your managing director may be tempted to use the press conference as an excuse for waxing lyrical about the joys of working for Joe's Widgets. Don't let him. You must be firm: only field your best speakers, and put them through a course of

Surviving the Media Jungle

presentation skills if you have to. No matter how many speakers you have – and it's usual to have one to three – there should not be more than fifteen minutes of speech time. Work on an average of 5 minutes per person. If you let your speakers rabbit on, you've killed your conference.

After the speeches, you may run your short video clip or audio-visual presentation, with the emphasis as always on the short. You should also budget time for a question and answer session before refreshments. Q+A sessions are often mixed bags. I have seen some which were well handled and some which went completely out of control. Journalists must ask questions – that's why they are there – but the sessions need to be directed. You need a chairman who ensures that everyone gets a fair go.

One of the worst Q+A sessions I attended was a press conference to launch a new portable phone. One journalist asked technical question after technical question, most of which went completely over the head of the generalist press who were present. Faced with someone like that, it is better to invite him to speak to you later, when you can answer his questions at length, rather than hold up everyone else. Q+A sessions should ideally last about 15 minutes, and you will know they have worked when there is a pleasant-sounding 'buzz' as the journalists file out of the room.

It is of paramount importance to display or demonstrate the product to its best advantage. You can impart valuable information via display boards, and 'themed' displays are also effective. A jeweller launching a new range of exotic necklaces, ear-rings and pendants from India created a mini-exhibition in his showroom, with models dressed in saris wearing the jewels, and other precious stones draped on silk cushions and rugs in glass cases; chairs and sofas were Indian in design, and Indian food was served.

When Matsushita launched the 'Squarial' satellite dish, it created a video wall with more than twenty different TV channels in several different languages playing at once. The wall was displayed in a mock-up of a typical British suburban living-room – a very effective demonstration.

Better still, get the press to try out the product for themselves. With food and drink, this is easily done – a sampling table can be set up, and give-aways included in the press 'goody-bag' if you choose to have one. With other products participation is more difficult. Exclusive Cars, however, could arrange for the press to test-drive its replica MG-A, or have a chauffeur-driven fleet outside the reception area giving rides to invited guests.

The best product demonstrations are usually the simplest. Beware of being too clever, or you might come unstuck. One DIY chain launched a new range of kitchen units, and journalists were invited to 'Build a Kitchen in 30 Minutes'. The press did not take kindly to lugging bits of plywood and Formica around, and as the assembly of the units was less simple than intimated by the instruction manual, the DIY manufacturer defeated his own objective.

The same criteria apply when using celebrities or some kind of floor show or entertainment. As we have seen, only use a celebrity if he is linked to or enhances your product. The States of Jersey frequently call on the actor John Nettles, who plays the Jersey detective Bergerac in the popular TV series, when they hold conferences, and

Surviving the Media Jungle

he has done much to increase tourist revenue for the Island.

But a singing-and-dancing, all-girl spectacular, complete with lasers and roller skates should only be contemplated if it is professionally produced. Nothing damages a company's reputation more than a shoddy, amateurish show that makes everyone a laughing stock. Such shows won't increase coverage. On the contrary, you may well find yourself gossiped about unfavourably in the *Daily Telegraph*'s Day By Day column, or the FT's Lex column!

When it comes to catering for a formal conference, remember the survey conducted by a catering company, which showed that 80 per cent of journalists were in favour of hot and cold buffet lunches at pressers. This gave them the opportunity of mingling with company personnel and other journalists, rather than being stuck at a single table. Naturally there will be times when formal sit-down receptions are mandatory. As always, the nature of the event dictates the format of the reception. It is also customary to offer journalists tea, coffee and biscuits on arrival. Catering staff should be personable, obliging and well-briefed: a friendly chat with the banqueting manager before the event will ensure all goes smoothly.

Teamwork is absolutely essential for the smooth running of a conference. Clear communication is vital: everyone concerned needs to know what everyone else is doing. Tasks should be individually assigned for the duration of the conference. Sometimes it's the simplest things which get overlooked.

Take, for example, the importance of starting on time. Many journalists complain that pressers start too late because the PROs are anxiously waiting for latecomers to arrive. There has to be a balance between waiting for the stragglers and keeping to the timetable. No press event should keep journalists hanging about for longer than 20 minutes. It's a matter of politeness as well as professionalism. And what about signs directing journalists round the venue? You may need these at strategic locations. Hotels and conference centres are notoriously bad at providing them, so you may well have to bring your own.

Then there's the press desk. It's important for the press to be welcomed by a smiling face. Who will be manning it? Do you need a visitors' book? Will you 'badge' the journalists as they come in? There's always a doubt as to whether you should 'label' the press. Personally I detest being badged, but I recognise how important it is for everyone to know who you are, and for you to know who everyone else is and what publication they are from. I prefer adhesive or Velcro-type labels to pinned labels: safety-pins can ruin suits. If you give your company personnel labels of a special colour, they can swiftly be identified.

On every press desk, there should be a standby press kit: this is a miraculous holdall which contains all the tiny little things you may have forgotten: extra labels, pens, sticky tape, Blu-tack, drawing pins, paper clips, scissors, extra press packs, blank slides, tent cards, writing paper, spare slide bulbs, plugs, aspirin. (You may need medication!)

Be sure the press bag is clearly marked as such. I remember the fatal day when a client and I had identical black bags. Mine contained the press kit, his contained slides for a presentation he was giving in Paris that

Surviving the Media Jungle

evening. After the conference the inevitable happened – and, like a scene from a Feydeau farce, I walked off with his case and he with mine. It took 2 hours before the mistake was discovered, and I had to courier the bag to a frantically Valium-popping client in Paris. You are duly warned!

Press packs should also be available for journalists, and they act as useful backgrounders to the event. Packs should contain:

- a press release on the event
- photograph(s) of product and key company executives
- background information on the company
- any other relevant information

Different PR writers have different ideas as to when you should give out press packs. Some say at the *end* of the conference, because juggling a press pack, glass of vino and canapés in one hand is difficult, and nothing is more distracting to speakers than a gaggle of pressmen shuffling papers during the conference itself.

I disagree because (a) no one says you have to hold the press packs in your hand anyway – most journalists have briefcases. (b) they don't need to rustle the papers when people are talking – in any case most journalists use the backs of the press packs to write their notes on, so they're invaluable journalistic tools. (c) I've conducted a survey, and every journo I spoke to liked getting a press pack *before* the conference started, just in case they're called away unexpectedly, and forgot to take one on their way out. So give them out at the beginning.

The look of the press pack is also important. It doesn't

need to be over-elaborate, and often a plain cardboard folder with the company logo emblazoned upon it is all that is required. Plastic wallets can also be used, but they do tend to look cheap and nasty. The best press-pack folders are stylish but unobtrusive, and the contents should reflect the nature of the press conference, and help the journalist write his story.

Goody-bags can be given out as the journalists are leaving. Again such gifts or mementoes are not essential, but if they help 'sell' the product to the press, then they have their place. When a leading manufacturer of packeted soups launched a new range, each journalist received a sample pack of every variety. Fair enough. But over-extravagant gifts – a year's supply of vouchers to a department store or free airline tickets – could be misconstrued or seen as a bribe. And you don't want to get into the 'pen, deskset, calendar, diary' syndrome. Better not to give a gift at all than to waste money on me-too giveaways like these.

Once the conference is over, your work is still not done. You should check your attendance list or visitors' book, and immediately mail press packs to journalists who did not attend. Inform your press-cutting service how much coverage you are likely to get and which papers to cut for. You may also have had requests for extra information from journalists which you need to progress; and once the stories have appeared, you can use them as a peg to telephone the press and find out if they require any other information. Pressers have multiple functions.

The best press conferences are the ones where everything has been planned to the last detail, but which look effortless and hardly stage-managed at all. Naturally this

Surviving the Media Jungle

NATIONAL SERVICE (ARMED FORCES INVITATIONS) ACT, 1939

YOU SHOULD TAKE **NOTICE OF INVITATION**
THIS NOTICE
WITH YOU WHEN
YOU REPORT

MINISTRY OF PUBLISHING AND NATIONAL SERVICE
EMPLOYMENT EXCHANGE

Divisional Office
25 Berkeley Square
London, W1X 6AB
Date: 11th July 1989

....
Features Editor
....

Registration No. WW2 1939/45

DEAR SIR/MADAM

I have to inform you that in accordance with the National Service (Armed Forces Invitations) Act, you are required to present yourself on 17th day August 1989 at 6.30pm, or as early as possible thereafter on that day, to celebrate the publication by Reader's Digest of <u>WORLD AT ARMS</u> at:—

Imperial War Museum
Lambeth Road
London, SE1
Elephant and Castle ....(nearest underground station)

If you wear glasses, please bring them with you. Kit should not exceed an overcoat (if cold), umbrella (if wet), briefcase (if working) and personal effects such as razor, hair brush, tooth brush, etc (if planning to stay in town overnight).

Immediately on receipt of this notice, you should inform Corporal Fiona Munro at the Reader's Digest HQ, 25 Berkeley Square, London W1X 6AB (01-629 8144, ext 6140), whether you are able to report for the party.

Yours faithfully,

R Hosie

Sgt R Hosie RAEC
for Divisional Controller

NB1   The Glenn Miller Orchestra will be on parade from 6.15pm.

NB2   The Hon Admiral of the Association of Dunkirk Little Ships will take the Parade.

NB3   Rations will be provided.

(19689) 0927423776 KE0300 4N

BRING ON THE GIN AND TONIC

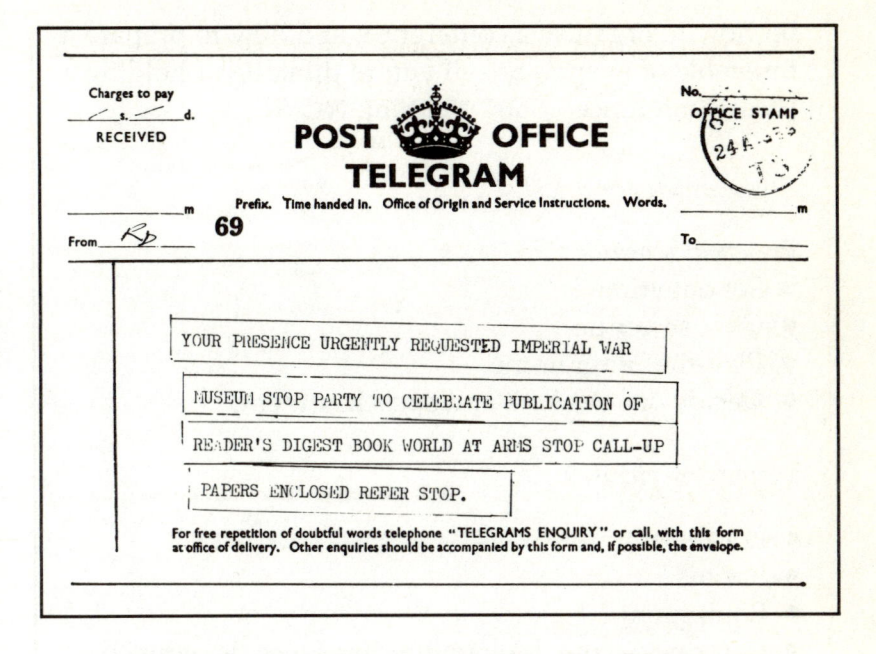

```
POST OFFICE TELEGRAM
Charges to pay ... RECEIVED ...
Prefix. Time handed in. Office of Origin and Service Instructions. Words.
69
From Rb                                         To

YOUR PRESENCE URGENTLY REQUESTED IMPERIAL WAR
MUSEUM STOP PARTY TO CELEBRATE PUBLICATION OF
READER'S DIGEST BOOK WORLD AT ARMS STOP CALL-UP
PAPERS ENCLOSED REFER STOP.
```

The difficulty with grabbers is treading the tightrope between irritating journalists, making the press groan and making them laugh: this one doesn't take itself too seriously and works as a result.

entails a great deal of work and effort from the team concerned. But at the end it's worth it, for a good presser creates goodwill and should generate the right sort of coverage.

The following checklist should give you a head-start

On the page opposite is an excellent grabber – sure to make a journalist smile. When *Reader's Digest* launched its book *World at Arms*, it invited the press by enclosing each journalist's 'Call-up Papers' on official M.O.D. stationery and in the right period style. The whole atmosphere of the 40s was recreated, including the Glenn Miller Orchestra playing 'In the Mood'.

[141]

Surviving the Media Jungle

on how to organise a conference, and how to prepare a timetable of events. So – if you're thinking of holding a press conference – start planning NOW!

Press conference checklist

Pre-event schedule
- Set date/time.
- Choose venue.
- Plan the programme.
- Decide on speakers and speech content.

Venue considerations

- Location.
- Rooms.
- Equipment.
- Catering – the banqueting manager is your best friend.

Other tasks

- Consider design and print requirements.
- Book a photographer.
- Allocate 'on the day' responsibilities.

Countdown: C-day minus one

- Phone press.
- Confirm details with venue administration and catering.
- REHEARSE, REHEARSE, REHEARSE.
- Finalise collateral.
- SET THE ALARM CLOCK!

On the day

- ARRIVE EARLY.
- Rehearse.
- Check equipment.
- Advise venue of last-minute alterations.
- Put up directional signs.
- Arrange press desk.
- Book messengers/taxis.

Timings

9.30 – Set up room(s).
11.30 – Press arrive.
12.00 – Presentation.
12.20 – Question and answer session.
13.00 – Reception/lunch.
14.30 – Press leave.
15.00 – Strike set.

8

Over the airwaves

I have left the chapter on dealing with radio and television, both in placement and in how to handle media interviews, till now because the broadcast industry is a special case, and should be treated as such. This will no doubt please TV and radio producers and editors, who have known this all along anyway (egos proliferate in the world of broadcasting). It may be a truism, but I will repeat it nevertheless: *don't approach radio and television as you would the medium of print*. It's not just a question of NOT sending photographs to radio stations – although when I worked at the World Service, many a PR pic came across my desk – it's a question of accepting that screen and audio operate in a different way.

The first difference is obvious – *pace*. Newspapers lend themselves to leisurely pursuits. You can browse through them, skimming or reading in depth. The print medium needs time to be absorbed.

But radio and television move fast. News items last 2–3 minutes each, and interviews tend towards the short, sharp shock. The viewer or listener reacts accordingly – matching the swift pace, he flicks from channel to channel until he finds an arresting programme. (When did you last flick through ten different newspapers at once, even on a lazy Sunday morning?) This is particularly true

Surviving the Media Jungle

of radio: with no interesting pictures to root him to the spot, the listener is probably only half listening anyway, and doing something else at the same time, whether it's washing the dishes or washing the dog. Bore the listener, and you've lost your audience. Lose your audience, and you've lost your ratings. Lose your ratings, and you'll probably find your programme axed before you can say 'Marconi'.

Which brings us to the second difference between the media – *the entertainment factor*. When you buy your daily newspaper, your prime requirement is for information and explanation (unless you're a page 3 addict). When you switch on the telly at 8.00 pm, you want to relax at the end of a hard day at the office.

Have you wondered why national dailies have a larger circulation than evening papers? In the morning you're primed and ready to go, so hard news suits your mood; in the evening you're pooped, and all you want to do is flop in an armchair and be amused. Of course you want to catch up on developments on the day's news – but in a digestible form. That means uncomplicated, readily assimilated viewing and listening – with arresting content.

Perhaps that's one of the reasons why the PR industry has treated the broadcast industry with some caution, and that records of placement have not been as high as in the print world. To turn a PR story into a surefire hit that grabs radio and television with irresistible sounds and pictures does not necessarily come naturally to businessmen, trained in logical thinking, facts and figures. Easier by far to write the story down on paper and mail it to the print medium.

Besides, newspapers have such a long pedigree, and

you can feel them, touch them, even smell the ink. Television and radio are mere upstarts in comparison, and much less tactile; even with cassette copies of interviews, which you can play back on tape or video recorders, you can't replace the solidity of a cuttings book, which can be sent to a client. In addition broadcasters do tend to get stroppy with PROs – most public relations people complain of the 'rudeness' they find amongst radio and TV journalists.

A lot of that has to do with the fast pace of broadcast material, and the bitchiness of the world in which most broadcasters move (with three colleagues about to stab you in the back, the last thing you care about is being *nice* to people). It helps to understand the way they work, but the best way to colonise the airwaves is to offer TV people pictures they can't ignore, and radio people sounds they can only get from *you*.

Broadcast placement

As with any story, you have to apply the Big Deal test ruthlessly when you're dealing with radio and television. If you're convinced you have a story, you then have to sell it in. But to whom?

Many well-meaning souls think that the right person to contact is the presenter of the programme. Very rarely. Presenters, however well-known, are often mere mouthpieces for other people's scripts. There are very few Esther Rantzens, who write the script, produce and present their own series, and have an active say in what the programme contents will be. In most cases the

Surviving the Media Jungle

decision-making process lies behind the cameras and microphones.

Although TV and radio are different from each other in many ways, their administrative structure is fairly similar. Most stations divide their programming into several neat units, each completely autonomous and self-directing:

- News and current affairs.
- Science and features.
- Music and arts.
- Documentary features.
- Light entertainment.
- Sport.
- Drama.

News and current affairs would cover programmes as diverse as ITV's *This Week* or Radio 4's *Today*, as well as such topical newsy programmes as *Woman's Hour*.

Science and features would cover such programmes as *Tomorrow's World*.

Music and arts include programmes such as *The South Bank Show*.

Documentary features would cover such programmes as *40 Minutes* or *Holiday*.

Light entertainment encompasses all comedy, game shows, sitcoms.

Sport and drama are self-explanatory.

Within these units there is a strictly observed hierarchy of management, and within both radio and television the pecking order looks something like this:

- Heads of departments.
- Commissioning editors.
- Producer(s).
- Reporter(s)/Presenter(s).
- Researcher(s).
- Production assistant(s).

Heads of departments, as their names suggest, are the seats of power, with the right to hire and fire, oversee on-air schedules, and create broadcast tactics for rateable programmes. They are usually former producers, with a great deal of production experience and a sound knowledge of the broadcast industry.

Commissioning editors are responsible for individual series of programmes, such as *Panorama* or *The Natural World*. They will be ultimately responsible for agreeing programme outlines, staffing for each programme within a series, budgets, and forward planning. A commissioning editorial post is considered a producer's promotion, and highly coveted.

Producers put programmes together. They come up with the ideas, choose the team, define the story-line and the content, edit the highlights, and are generally responsible for getting a product on-air. Working to commissioning editors, they will be responsible for one or more programmes within a series, depending on scope and budget. More often than not, producers are former programme researchers, although occasionally

Surviving the Media Jungle

reporting staff turn to hands-on production. From a PR point of view it's vital to have producers on one's side.

Reporters/Presenters. Once a reporter, always a reporter – there's a buzz to the news that makes few reporters and journalists want to give up the thrill of helping to make news happen. Working directly with research and production staff, reporters tell it as it is, and coordinate story-lines and news angles. They will interpret a producer's view of a story and focus attention on identified issues.

Few presenters have the clout of reporters. They will write their scripts to a limited degree, but most are simply figureheads with pleasant faces or voices, mouthing the words of others. There are of course notable exceptions to the rule, as we have seen: the Brian Redheads and Sue McGregors of broadcasting are an integral part of the production process. But in most cases the presenter is the least likely person to help you in your quest for broadcast publicity, with opinions carrying little weight.

Researchers. Working directly to producers, researchers are the programme 'runners' – they will gather lists of suitable locations and interviewees, help create programme ideas, research background information for producers, reporters and presenters. They are often chosen for their in-depth knowledge of a particular subject, which can prove invaluable in series creation, e.g. most researchers on a programme on China will know the country well, and probably speak Chinese. Most researchers are keen to take on direct production, and promotion for them is a producer's post. They are key production opinion-formers, and should be courted.

Production assistants. In television PAs are glorified secretaries, typing up scripts, booking location recording equipment, co-ordinating schedules, soothing fevered brows. Like many secretaries, they are often overworked, underpaid and underestimated. Production assistants dream of going up a notch and becoming researchers. Some achieve this ambition. Most don't. Needless to say, most PAs are women.

In radio, however, the term PA is sometimes synonymous with 'studio manager' or 'engineer', and many PAs are found in studio, working directly with producers to edit programmes. They are skilful sound editors, and lead a varied life, working on a number of different programmes and projects daily. It's a creative career path – many PAs become programme producers.

As you can see, your first step to broadcast placement of a story will be to convince the researchers or producers. You will find that on national radio and television programmes the researchers are the first point of contact. On smaller stations, with smaller budgets and fewer staff, producers are often their own researchers, and become the main contact points.

It's a good idea to be familiar with the programme format before you sell in the story. Is the programme hard or soft, current affairs or features? How does the story-line on your product or service fit in with that concept? If it doesn't tally, can you alter the angle to suit?

Remember that stills for your own corporate video may make useful background material for TV, if the video has been shot to broadcast standard on 1" tape (BVU). But if this is not appropriate, bear in mind that

Surviving the Media Jungle

camera crews and reporters will probably wish to pre-record, often on your factory or office premises.

Talk over their requirements with the researcher: you may need to provide extra lighting, a room far from the madding crowd for interviews, even fax and phone facilities, especially if the story is a hot one. As we've already found out in Chapter 7 on press conferences, if the press is turning up on your doorstep, don't let your staff be the last to know!

If camera crews turn up, it's worth while badging your staff so that the company name is clearly visible, or ensuring that somehow your company's name or product is on display. Don't go over the top: producers hate puffery, and if they can cut out a frame with a bit of free advertising in it, they will. So try and liaise with the crews and convince them that the shot with your factory in the background offers the best vantage point, or that the product must be shown during the interview.

One of the best PR stunts I saw was arranged by Bejam, which was working with a London council to recondition old fridges with non-CFC, ozone-friendly cooling systems. A Bejam engineer, with company logo emblazoned on his overalls, was shown on both BBC and Thames television, working on a 1960s fridge. The reporter on-air only mentioned that 'a freezer company' was doing its bit – but the logo was there for all to see.

One of the problems with audio material is that such visible product plugs cannot be engineered, so it's up to you, somehow, to describe your company and product in such a way that it is perfectly obvious to the listener who or what you are talking about. On a *Woman's Hour* programme I compiled about the state of the British shoe industry, I was forbidden by my producer, on pain of death, to introduce one of my interviewees as a buyer from Marks and Spencer. She was introduced as a buyer 'from one of Britain's major high-street chains'. Not to be foxed, the buyer neatly sidestepped the problem by stating that 'thousands of pairs of shoes, *wrapped in our distinctive bright green shopping bags*, are sold in our stores every day'. That's ingenuity.

Media interviews

Interviews offer businessmen an unparalleled opportunity to get a corporate message across with immediacy, and to the right audience. But interviews must be handled with care, and that means understanding a few basic dos and don'ts.

Let's take the print medium first. One-to-one meetings, as we have seen, are excellent means to an end: the journalist gets to know about the way you work, and you get to know his interests, specific areas of expertise, and the needs of his newspaper or magazine.

Unless the journalist is known to be a hard-liner with a particular axe to grind (in which case it's up to you whether you talk to him or not), most print interviews are fairly relaxed affairs. You have time to talk, to express your views, to question the reporter. Print interviews are the best chance you have of putting your best case forward, so take advantage of them.

But broadcast programming is a very different affair, whether you're being recorded live, pre-recorded, or taking part in a phone-in or live-link-up by satellite. You have very little time to put your point of view across, and

Surviving the Media Jungle

the message you leave behind has to be succinct enough to stand alone and not be edited out, if you're pre-recorded; strong enough to compete with other points of view and other interviews if you're going out live.

Added to that there's the alienating factor of having to go into a radio or television studio, which is daunting in itself; plus the horror of hearing your own voice played back to you, and seeing your mugshot on the screen. Few people like what they see, and most detest what they hear.

Noses look bigger and frames look fatter on TV; plummy accents can break glass on radio, and Glaswegians can come across as incomprehensible. Some people are so put off by the impression they think they leave behind that they decide there and then that once is enough, and never go through the ordeal again. Which is a pity – because, mostly, all it takes is a little practice, and an understanding of what the media want.

What do they want? Simple. If a television or radio programme has got in touch with you, it's because a researcher or producer has spotted a potential story. It may not necessarily be the kind of story you want to hear, but your name has been pulled out of a hat or you have been recommended by a colleague as a subject worthy of an interview. If they approach you, you can always turn them down. But consider the following points:

- If you refuse, they may offer the interview to your nearest rival.

- The interview may give you a unique chance to state your case to millions of listeners and viewers.

- They may never approach you again, and you may have lost a good opportunity for furthering media contacts.

- Whether you like it or not, your refusal to participate or appear may sound as if you have something to hide. The term 'no comment' implies guilt, resulting in the twitching of a thousand eyebrows and many knowing smiles.

If you genuinely can't co-operate – you may be out of the country, or at another meeting – then tell them so, making sure they know that you would like to help out in the future. But if you can appear, then do so. You'll probably find it's not as painful as you thought.

What to expect: Radio

One of the first things to remember is that there is a great deal of difference between local and national radio. There are thirty-eight BBC and sixty-one ILR stations in the UK, and more to come as the Broadcasting Bill ushers in a new era of community broadcasting, with a fifth national channel, and Greek and Tamil Radio on the horizon. Local radio stations are usually small and friendly, and there's a refreshing air of informality. The premises themselves may be a converted barn or an old warehouse – sometimes the reception area actually backs on to the studio.

BBC stations tend to be a quieter mode of delivery – perhaps a throwback to Lord Reith – with a strong emphasis on news and community affairs. There's still a

Surviving the Media Jungle

good deal of talk and comment, with music sandwiched in between.

Independent stations tend towards the reverse: news bulletins are shorter, snappier, and there's a raunchy, punchy style; talk is sandwiched in between music. News is 'drip-fed' to locals via Independent Radio News coming from the capital. But even on an all-news station such as LBC in London, news is delivered in cloudbursts that match the mood of commuters: fast and furious, with little time to breathe. *If you're interviewed on independent radio, remember that listeners want a brief outline rather than an in-depth discussion, and the tone is chattier.*

National BBC radio moves at a more sedate pace: it's not that the news is any slower in arriving, it's just that it's handled differently. There's a greater tendency to analyse and comment, and questions tend to be more searching. On a news programme such as *The World Tonight* you may well find yourself interviewed by one of the country's leading broadcasters, and that could be a little awe-inspiring. Feature-based programmes are generally pre-recorded and more relaxed: you will have more time to think about what you want to say, change your mind and go over your questions again.

But there's no doubt that walking into main reception at Broadcasting House does give you a feeling of being at the heart of things. Perhaps it's the friezes on the walls, solemnly stating that 'nation shall speak unto nation'.

If you're interviewed on national radio, listeners will be expecting fuller answers to fuller questions, delivered in a more formal way. I'm not saying that you should go all po-faced at the Beeb, and do a song-and-dance routine on independent; but there is a difference in emphasis and style which you should be aware of.

What to expect: Television

All regional television stations across the country – and there are fifteen independent and eight BBC currently – are 'fed' by a national news output: Independent Television News (ITN) for the independents, and central BBC news desks. Added to this, stations put forward their own local news programmes, after the main bulletins during the day and evening.

Regional stations also supply a small amount of programming on drama and documentaries for national distribution. They are intensely proud of this, and of their regional output. Smaller TV stations feel the competition of larger, more affluent stations very keenly. Egos abound in television, and there is a great deal of posturing, from the glamorous receptionist, desperate to become a presenter, to the harassed floor managers and researchers, desperate to oust the current series producer.

Remember that your likelihood of being interviewed for television is lower than it would be for radio, because there are far more local radio stations than TV stations, so that their hunger for news is greater. Moreover TV can of course use means other than the interview for getting the message across, such as footage of your premises overlaid with a reporter's voice-track.

However, regional magazine programmes are often on the look out for local stories, which may well give your company a chance, and if you have to go into studio, remember that, unlike radio, *there is little difference in emphasis between BBC and independent stations as regards the style of news*. You have to get your message over as briefly and concisely as possible, and because the cameras are on you, you must look and sound both authoritative and humane.

The studios

Radio

Many writers on the media state that radio stations are more distracting than TV studios. I disagree. Having worked in both, I find TV studios much more alienating and chaotic.

Your first contact at a radio station will probably be the PA or researcher, who will greet you and take you to the studio. If you have time before you go on air, you will probably meet the producer of the programme, who will fill you in on how the programme will run, and the programme's presenter, if he or she is still not on air. There may be time to relax with a cup of coffee, and also time to 'suss' the programme atmosphere. If you can ask the presenter or producer about the outline of questioning you will be expected to answer, you should have a fair idea of what to expect. That's why it's a good idea to get to studio at least 30 minutes before you're due to go on air, because you will be able to take a deep breath, familiarise yourself with your surroundings, and get those nerves under control.

The studio itself is often hidden away, and if you're interviewed at Broadcasting House, you'll probably be taken down to the basement, where the studios nestle one against the other like mini air-raid shelters. You'll find the room will be divided in two: behind a glass window will sit the producer and the studio manager, fiddling with tape-decks and equipment; on the other side there will be a table, probably circular, and several chairs, with an enormous microphone opposite each. Most people hate having a mike that size under their nose, and it has thrown many an unsuspecting interviewee. Expect it, and you'll feel less daunted, because that is where and how you will sit, facing your interviewer. The important thing is to view the experience as a challenge, but not as a war.

Television

If a radio station is a bit like an air-raid shelter, then a TV studio is like an aircraft hangar. At first sight it appears bigger than it needs to be: wide open spaces filled with cameras and technicians, bright lights and loads of wires (watch your feet!). There are two reasons for the size: firstly, cameras need large floor space to manoeuvre into different angles; secondly, the programme you are going to be on is only one of a number of shows, each with its own set, which will be shot in that particular studio. Your own set area is actually quite small – a haven of familiarity among all the high-tech. A sofa and coffee table set-up does for a chat-show or informal discussion, and news desks and swivel chairs for current affairs type programmes. If you see the kind of chair they use for *Mastermind* being used, be warned: the programme is going to be a toughie, so expect a grilling!

Tucked away high up somewhere lies the control room, with producers, directors and other studio staff who put the programme together, relaying messages to the presenters/reporters via ear-pieces.

Sit down and make yourself comfortable. Your microphone is a tiny clip-on, which you'll hardly even notice

Surviving the Media Jungle

(unlike radio's gi-normous affair.) The presenter will probably be sitting next to you, chummily, the idea being to make viewers at home think the screen is an extension of their living-room. Such artificial bonhomie will not be reflected by the attitude of the TV staff.

Look around you. Everyone seems to be running around in a panic – bustling floor managers with clipboards, the make-up lady powdering your nose at the last minute before you go on-air, the researcher requesting updates on information . . . TV stations appear busy even when nothing is happening, and there's a sense of urgency even to the most innocuous programmes – a heightened tension that can be doubled if the programme is going out live.

Arrive early, if you can, to acclimatise yourself to the ambience of the studio. Before you go on air, you may well be invited to meet the producer or other guests informally in the Hospitality or Green Room. There will be lots to eat and drink. Beware! Alcohol is the snare of the feckless interviewee. The time to relax is after the interview, not before. You may find yourself saying things you might regret, and letting slip bits of information that should remain secret.

Rule one of any interview is that there is no such thing as 'off the record', and you must never be off your guard until you are well clear of the building. Remember President Reagan's gaffe before a press conference, when the microphones were being tested for sound: 'We have just begun bombing the Soviet Union', he joked, unaware he was already being recorded. Enough said.

Training

If you're unsure how to handle any interview, whether it's print or broadcast, the first thing I would suggest is to get yourself or your company spokesman media-trained. There are many companies who specialise in passing on to businessmen the necessary techniques, and it's certainly worth the investment.

Those businesses that know how to deal with the media effectively are those that get their message across best, and come over as believable and trustworthy. You only need to look at how badly the Football Association handled questions regarding the Hillsborough football disaster to see how damaging poorly fielded questions can be to any organisation. The FA came across as unconcerned and even heartless, which has no doubt done it long-term damage.

This of course relates to crisis management, and there is no scope to deal with this at length in this book. But preparation for media handling of a crisis is often one of the best ways to handle a crisis in the first place, and a key management tool.

Similarly, if your company and/or its products have been singled out by an investigative programme such as *Watchdog*, and you need to defend yourself, you must know what to expect and how to handle the tough-talking questions an abrasive reporter will fling at you. Anticipation is the strongest form of self-defence you can have against the media. So if you have never considered media training, think very hard about it. There are many companies that can help you, and some are listed in Appendix I, pp. 204–5.

Surviving the Media Jungle

Techniques

Let's start with radio. The plus with radio is that you can have your notes with you and look at them from time to time during your interview, providing you don't make a noise as you shuffle papers around. That gives you a certain feeling of security. In addition you're not visible, so it really doesn't matter if you look like the Wicked Witch of the West, providing you've got something interesting to say.

One drawback with radio is that, because you're not visible, you can't show those little communicative gestures – nods, grimaces, smiles – that add animation to your conversation. Your voice will have to do all the acting for you. The best radio performers are the ones who realise that once on-air they have to show a heightened version of themselves to the listener.

On radio, the 'natural' you will probably come over sounding flat; a slightly more dramatic you will actually sound very natural. Notice I used the words 'radio performers'. We're back to the concept of broadcasting as entertainment, I'm afraid.

With no picture to see, the listener will automatically be drawn to a lively, colourful, well-modulated voice, with varied inflexions. It doesn't have to be standard BBC either – regional accents can be very attractive. But nothing works less than a boring, monotonous, anaesthetising voice. It's death on air.

You can practise by recording yourself on a cassette recorder at home. Listen carefully. How can you improve your performance? Try changing the emphasis on certain words – stressing the most important, lifting your inflexion slightly at the end of a sentence. Makes a difference, doesn't it? Remember that when you're next asked to go into the studio.

Women have another problem when it comes to broadcasting, and that's all to do with frequency. Women's voices are of course higher-pitched than men's, and that often plays havoc with the airwaves. Have you considered why the best female broadcasters have lower, sultrier voices? It's not a fluke – it just happens that deeper voices suit the airwaves better. Women also, when excited, have a tendency to squeak.

I know only too well – when broadcasting, I have to deliberately lower my own naturally high-pitched voice or I sound like an intoxicated Munchkin. And I'm in illustrious company: when Margaret Thatcher fought the 1979 election and won, she had learned to drop her voice by almost a full octave!

The second drawback to radio is those notes. If you read them, you will sound stilted and artificial. Unless you are an unsung Lawrence Olivier, it's very difficult to read convincingly. So don't bury yourself in your notes. Refer to them from time to time, but never depend on them.

Once you've got the voice under control, there's the microphone to worry about. It can be very off-putting. The secret is to try and ignore it: look your interviewer in the eye instead, get immersed in the conversation, and you should find you have forgotten about the mike.

The best radio comes across as a broadcaster talking directly to you, the listener. It's not easy to achieve that one-to-oneness and immediacy. But take a tip from the professionals: one of the secrets of good radio is to imagine a special listener to whom you are speaking. Don't broadcast to the world, broadcast to a single indi-

Surviving the Media Jungle

vidual – it can be your wife, boy friend, mother or best friend, but imagine that one person in your mind. You'll find that thinking of that person 'humanises' your delivery, and helps you concentrate. John Arlott, the famous cricket commentator and wine correspondent, imagines his son sitting in the chair opposite him. It certainly works for him. It's a technique you can use for TV too – broadcast to a single viewer.

Another tip is never to drum your fingers or tap the table – the microphones are so sensitive, they will pick up and intensify the weeniest sound, and even the slightest rustle of papers will sound like a whiplash. Politicians who pound their fists when they are talking are sheer agonies to the studio managers, who have to, somehow, reduce the decibels to a level acceptable to listeners. (To this day I cringe when the uninitiated 'test' mikes at press conferences or other functions by *blowing* into them – horrors! – or howling 'testing one-two-three . . .' The best way to test a mike is to scratch it very softly with your thumbnail.)

Jangly ear-rings and clunky bracelets are also to be avoided. If you toss your head, it will sound like hell breaking loose in the china department of Harrods.

With television you have all of this and more to think about. As we have seen, cameras intensify personal idiosyncracies – little smiles can look like smirks, the odd raised eyebrow can appear to be a nervous twitch. The best thing is to try and forget what you look like, and concentrate on what you're saying.

When it comes to what to wear, that's fairly easy: unless you're a fashion designer, or someone in the arts for whom outrageous clothes are part of your TV message, pick a conservative suit or dress that enhances your own professionalism. Avoid colours such as straight black and white or red, which don't reproduce well on screen; or stripes and checks, which 'move around', almost blinding the viewer with their strobe effect.

Accept make-up if it's offered – and it probably will be. Unless you want to look as if you're suffering from some incurable disease, a little spot of Leichner never did anyone any harm. This rules applies to ladies too: don't expect your street make-up to be enough. TV make-up is specifically designed for the medium, and very different from normal day-to-day wear.

Now how to sit. Look alert. Nothing is more off-putting than a seemingly lazy body lolling in a chair. Pundits even say that Neil Kinnock lost the 1987 election by appearing too casual and laid-back on screen, whereas Mrs Thatcher sat bolt upright, brimming with vitality. I'm not saying you have to imitate Mrs T – but it illustrates a point.

Perch yourself on the edge of your seat, and look your interviewer in the eye. You'll automatically feel more confident and in control. Try and forget the cameras, the technicians, or any monitors slung above your head (*nothing* clams you up more than actually seeing yourself on screen as you are talking). The best way to reach the viewer is to talk directly to your interviewer. *And be yourself*.

Unless you suffer from the Jonathan Miller syndrome – five hands talking when two will do – gestures and the odd mannerism won't detract from your performance. In fact you will probably come across as very natural, which you won't do if your hands hang stiffly by your sides. Speak clearly, letting every point sink in, and *use language everyone can understand*. Jargon is an inter-

Surviving the Media Jungle

viewee's worst enemy. It's like press release writing all over again: what seems normal everyday language to you will be totally alien to the average viewer. If you're using an unfamiliar term, explain it in layman's terms.

One of the things I find very irritating about some interviews is the laboured chumminess of presenter and guest – on first-name terms before the cameras whirr. I'm not a fan of using first names for interviewers you don't know, and I think it comes across as phony and unbelievable. In any case it's not the interviewer you want to reach, but the viewer. If you want to appear friendly and approachable, better by far to do so through your own way of talking: use colourful language, similes, metaphors or anecdotes if you can. This humanises the interview and brings immediacy to the viewer.

Think laterally. Facts are important, but don't talk of something being '3.2 microns' in length, but 'the size of a pin-head'; don't refer to '48 hectares of rain-forest destroyed every hour' but to 'rain-forests the size of Wembley stadium'. Support your statements by language the viewer can relate to.

As for notes, you will be constantly tempted to read them, and the fact that they are there can be distracting. But if you have to have notes, the best are two or three key points written down on a postcard, but no more. Fiddling about with folders and files looks messy and unprofessional, and the last impression you want to leave behind is of someone who doesn't know what he is talking about.

If you're discussing a company product, a good idea is to bring the product along with you to the studio, if it's small enough or easily transportable, and refer to it during the interview. Pointing to and discussing a product which is in front of you brings the interview to life, and makes your task a lot easier. You're also on familiar territory, and the very fact of touching and talking about something you know well should ease the nerve factor.

Ah, those nerves! How to deal with them? The first thing to say is that being nervous is no bad thing – any actor will tell you that pre-performance butterflies actually enhance the performance by getting the adrenalin to flow. If you're not nervous at all, you may not turn in your best. (This is why so many opening nights in the theatre are a roaring success and second nights are notorious disasters!).

So turn your nervous energy into speaker energy and let it help you through the interview. However, butterflies are one thing – petrification quite another. To help you relax, it's a very good idea to take deep breaths during the minutes before the interview. Concentrate purely on the physical act of breathing, think about anything you like *except the interview*. This should not only calm you down but oxygenate the brain, and make your mental responses that much sharper.

If you happen to be a chronic nerve-clam, there are many other techniques around, such as meditation and the proven Alexander Technique, which is available in course form at many institutions. It doesn't matter what you choose, providing it works for you. Artificial aids, such as Beta-Blockers to calm you down, should be the very last resort, and taken only after consultation with your physician.

But however nervous you are, if you know your facts and have a few choice phrases at your fingertips, nothing should go wrong.

Surviving the Media Jungle

Content

If you have agreed to appear on television or radio, you have obviously a sound business reason for doing so. The following points will help you put yourself across.

Determine your objectives first. What do you want to say to the viewers or listeners? How do you want your company and its products to be perceived? What impression do you want to leave behind?

Then determine the objectives of the programme. Look at things from the broadcasters' viewpoint. Why have they contacted you in the first place? What's in it for them? What's the story? What kind of angle will the producer be trying to put forward? Be prepared to face a negative stance from the programme. Bad news sells copy and programmes, after all.

Get to know the programme well. If at all possible, preview the show before going on. Get a feel for the style. Is it a 'hard' news format like *Horizon* or *This Week*, or softer? Does the programme have a political or other axe to grind?

Anticipate the line of questioning. Journalists are in the business of creating informative, intriguing, often controversial programmes. So – what sort of questions would you expect to be asked? Write down the answers you would give, and know your story backwards. Don't let yourself be caught out. Ask yourself the sensitive/

nasty question you don't want to be asked and find an answer to it. If necessary, consult your company chairman to make sure you are giving out the company line. But don't give yourself enough rope to hang yourself with by simply answering 'no comment'.

A former chairman of British American Tobacco was once asked on-air, by a *Panorama* interviewer, 'If you believed smoking were harmful to health, would you change your marketing policies?' He refused to answer the question, and it is no coincidence that he is no longer chairman of BAT. My company is often called in to advise corporations whose spokesmen fidget about uncomfortably when asked hot potato questions by the press. Our advice has always been to come up with a corporate message, sometimes allied to other leaders in their industry. It's always best to comment from as wide a viewpoint as possible. Truth convinces, lies are dangerous and will be sniffed out by the press, and evasion is downright deadly. Never bluff. If you really don't know, say so – and add you'll get back and find out as soon as you can.

Rehearse your answers with a member of your team. It's a fallacy to think you can be over-prepared for interviews. The truth is you can never be over-rehearsed. Get your wife, boss, partner, to put you through your paces until you feel confident about your answers. The interview itself may go down a slightly different path, but if you have thought it through properly, you should be fairly confident about the end result. You'll also find that if you have rehearsed properly, the dummy-runs will be probably worse than the real thing, and you should simply breeze through your interview.

Surviving the Media Jungle

Summarise the points you want to make in two or three hard-hitting key phrases. With only 2 or 3 minutes to get your point of view across, it's unlikely you will have time to launch into vast panegyrics about your company's market share and your hopes for worldwide expansion. Think of the two or three main features benefits of your company or product that you want to get over during the interview, and write them down – that way, you'll be sure to remember them. No matter what line of questioning you will be given, keep on referring back to those points. This ensures that even if you are pre-recorded, and therefore easy to edit, your main points will be difficult to cut out entirely.

Nor is there any need to limit your answers to the main-line question. Take control. Use questions as a springboard. Politicians do this all the time. How many times have you heard an MP say: 'That's a very interesting question about inflation. But you know my views on this. What I'd really like to talk about is our attitude towards the single European market.' Do the same. Change questions to your advantage if you can.

Be positive – and turn negatives into positives. Your product is not 'an expensive rip-off' – it offers 'quality and value for money'. It's not a 'useless device' – it appeals to 'a special interest group', and so on. There's a flip-side to every negative question – search it out. What you want viewers to remember is the good news about your product. Don't repeat negative questioning either. If an interviewer says 'You're going to close down three factories, aren't you?', don't answer 'No, we're not going to close down three factories, our plans are . . .', because an audience will remember the negatives in preference to the positives. Answer 'Certainly not. In fact we plan to remodel our existing premises over the next few years'.

If the news is decidedly black – say you are a manufacturer of contaminated yoghurt which has given rise to an outbreak of botulism – show your company's concern for the individuals affected and state what your company is going to do to prevent such outbreaks in the future. Stress your company's excellent track record and your desire to serve your customers well in the future. Don't gloss over the bad news – but make sure viewers and listeners understand that you are a responsible company and that you have matters well under control.

Never attack the media. You won't stand a chance. One of the first rules of media relations is that the media nearly always score the final point. A cool, controlled, well-briefed spokesman who handles negative questioning deftly comes across the best.

If the media have got their facts wrong – tell them. If you don't have the evidence to support your case on you, tell them you will find it and show them later. Don't let them get away with errata, but verbal abuse is no way to get your message across. When John Nott, then Secretary of State for Defence, memorably pulled his microphone off during an interview with Sir Robin Day, complaining 'I don't have to take this' and stormed out of the studio, he harmed his case irreparably.

Interviewer types

It's dangerous to assume that interviewers all come in

Surviving the Media Jungle

the same shapes and sizes. They don't. Apart from such obvious differences as sex and age, they have varied styles and individual techniques. You can be assaulted in a number of subtle, and not so subtle, ways.

The leading public relations company Burson-Marsteller operates its own media-training department, and in the UK trains more than 1,000 companies each year on interview techniques. It has put together an amusing but fairly factual summary of the many interviewer 'types' and how to deal with them, and I have reproduced them here.

The machine gunner is quite a pain. He will fire several questions at you at once – 'why are you such an unsuccessful company? Aren't you trying to hide the fact that you're fighting a take-over? How do you explain your loss of £35.2 million last year?' The way to deal with this kind of aggressive questioning technique is to answer only one question: the one which fits your message closest. After this, your questioner will simply follow on from your last point – interviewing after all, follows a logical sequence.

The interrupter is rude. He will stop you from finishing your sentence, and cut in before you have made your point. Refuse to be flurried. Stop him by cutting in yourself: 'I will answer your question in a moment, but I must finish what I was going to say'. Once again, take a tip from the politicians – they never let anyone barge in without a fight!

The paraphraser likes to simplify your statements by abbreviation, but this often leads to inaccuracy. Don't let words be put into your mouth, and if the paraphrase is not correct, say so.

The dart-thrower is sneaky. He jollies you along, and just as you think the interview is going well, he throws in a deadly question – 'I'm glad your pharmaceutical company has increased its turnover, but what's all this about aluminium in the antacids you produce?' The rule here is never be over-confident about an interview, and always be prepared to meet the unexpected. Journalists will try and surprise you if they can.

The good mate is a dart-thrower in disguise. He'll be cheery and jokey, and will try and make you feel so relaxed that you will have dropped your guard before you know it. Especially in pre-recorded situations, this kind of approach is lethal. He may offer you a cigarette or a drink, and you may be persuaded to discuss your company's performance 'off the record, just between us – we're not recording, as you can see . . .' Again remember there is *no such thing as off the record*. Once a reporter, always a reporter – and if he doesn't use your golden nuggets of information, he will trade them to a colleague who will. (It's worth while staying off the booze and fags during interviews too.)

The strong silent type. This is my definition, and the technique I personally like to use when interviewing. Ask a question – your interviewee will answer it. Then you pause. Nine times out of ten your interviewee continues to speak, simply to fill the silence. Many a beauteous clanger has been dropped thus. Then you pounce: you've got your prey. The secret of dealing with this kind

Surviving the Media Jungle

of interviewer is to remember that nature abhors a vacuum, and so does the public. If silence continues for too long, viewers and listeners will switch channels or switch off. So say what you want to say – and then shut up. It's the interviewer's job to ask the next question and fill that gap: let him get on with it!

Once you have finished your interview, the temptation is to tear off the microphone and leap out of your chair with a cry of relief and run out of the studio screaming: 'Thank God that's over!' Don't. The cameras may still be rolling, you may still be wired for sound. (Remember President Reagan again.) Wait until the producer or PA gives you the all clear.

That's all there is to it. You see? You've survived the media jungle. An unequalled opportunity to meet the press and the public was yours, and you took it. And the journalists were only doing their job, after all. It wasn't so bad. And next time, you'll feel all the more confident.

Next time . . . There's a lot you can do before next time. You can have your interview recorded and play it back. Criticise yourself constructively. What worked about your interview? Were there any real mistakes? How could you have improved? Did you come over as grim or unfriendly? You will probably be your own best critic. Similarly you will find that once you have been interviewed on radio or television, you will find yourself analysing interviews much more critically. Listening and watching others is a great way to learn.

But no matter what has been said in this chapter, perhaps the most important part is that you don't have to be a professional commentator. No one expects it of you.

OVER THE AIRWAVES

What the viewers and listeners want to see and hear is you – Joe Public, putting across your point of view, in your own particular way. Simply be yourself. And you'll do fine.

9

Beyond the press release

It's a mistake to think that the press release is the only way to get media coverage. There are many other PR tools you can use to reach a wide and targeted audience. Used in conjunction with traditional methods, they flesh out a media-relations campaign.

Many of these methods are broadcast-based, reflecting the growth in audio-visual communications that will become even more apparent over the next decade. Many of these 'aids to PR' have also been pioneered in the United States, and are only just becoming forces to be reckoned with in the UK. In PR terms we have always been about 5 years behind the US, and there is still a lot of groundwork to be done before many of these methods become accepted PR practice in the UK. However, they are here, and, used creatively, they provide a fresh dimension to the news-making process.

Media tours

When Farley Health Products relaunched its baby milks after the salmonella crisis in 1987, its public relations company organised a nationwide media tour for the

Surviving the Media Jungle

Farley spokesman, who was in this case a nurse specialising in the care of infants and young babies. The idea was to tell the whole country, via its regional media, that Farley was back, that Farley products were safe, and that mothers should have no fear about feeding Farley milks to their babies.

The itinerary was carefully planned to coincide with the product relaunch. The country was divided into media outlets – north, south, west and east – and a team of PROs hit the telephones. Contacting the main newspapers, radio and TV of each region, they talked to features editors, programme producers and researchers. Were they interested in an interview on baby care and infant feeding with a Farley spokesperson? No, this wasn't going to be a plug for Farley – but, yes, the products were soon to be back on the shelves, and they had been totally repackaged so they were absolutely safe.

The response was tremendous. Farley was a trusted and well-loved brand, and an institution in baby care. Everyone wanted to hear how the company had fought back and won, after the devastation that closing the Kendal factory had caused.

For two weeks the Farley nurse, accompanied by a public relations executive, toured the country, spreading the Farley Gospel. They spoke to regional newspapers and freesheets, were invited on to radio chat-shows and after-six regional news magazine programmes on television. In all cases the thrust of the interviews was present-day practice in infant feeding, but in each case the Farley comeback was clearly stated. This was not difficult to achieve: the Farley saga was, after all, a matter of national interest, and was a topical, newsworthy item.

The results were clear: the media tour had ensured

that there was nationwide awareness of the product relaunch, which was the identified objective. Media tours are exhausting, taking time to organise and very tiring to pursue, but they are the most immediate way I know of disseminating a message. Such tours do not have to be nationwide, either. You can choose the geographic areas relevant to your target market, and concentrate on them alone. But you need a willing and well-trained company spokesman, who has the time, talent and energy to devote 1 or 2 weeks to pure media activity. It is not always easy to find such a paragon of virtue, but the rewards are well worth it.

To set up a media tour, it is best to plan as follows:

- Identify media message(s) and select spokesman/ gimmick if appropriate.
- Identify target geographical areas and provisional timings for tour.
- Identify target media (print, radio or television, or a combination of all three).
- Sell-in story-line to target media and follow up by letter.
- Plot timetable.
- Book accommodation and make travel arrangements.
- Reconfirm week before travel begins.

That is the ultimate targeted message, but it has not yet become commonplace media activity. Perhaps it is because such a tour requires a great investment in terms of man-hours and personnel; and it is pointless arranging such a tour for a mere product launch, unless it happens to be a very rare and unusual product. The strength of the message is of paramount importance for the success of a media tour. Properly organised, however, it is hard to beat, and if you are keen to generate column-inches for your client, there is no better way.

Syndicated radio tapes

Syndicated radio tapes are used a great deal by public relations companies, and most misuse them. The concept is simple: an interview of about 3 minutes is recorded about a company and/or its products. The interview is copied and mailed out, or syndicated, to about thirty-five local radio stations, sometimes a mixture of BBC and independent stations, sometimes to ILR stations alone.

The client pays for the tape's production. The stations receive the recorded material for nothing, and play it at their discretion. Therein lies the rub: many such PR tapes are pure aural puffery, and a blatant excuse for product plugs and over-commercialism. They praise the product to the skies, and offer little feature value.

In consequence they are not used, and irritated news editors simply dump them in the wastepaper bin where they belong. But syndicated tapes *can* work if you remember some golden rules:

- *Make a tape that is truly interesting*, and that makes good radio listening.

BEYOND THE PRESS RELEASE

- *Don't over-plug the product.* Generalise the feature, and introduce the product name only once in 3 minutes (this is partly to comply with existing IBA regulations, and partly because mentioning the name only once avoids over-commercialising the tape.)
- *Have a USP.* Something must make your tape sound different to other syndicated material: unusual sound effects, celebrity interviewees, odd subject-matter, exotic locations. Make the producer who is listening to the tape *have* to use it.
- *Keep it regional.* Local radio stations, like newspapers, want local news. Find a local angle. It's not difficult to record a core tape with selected regional angles tagged on to the end for better placement.
- *Sports, charities and funnies are winners.* Programme-makers like to use tapes about sports events they can't cover themselves, and tapes about good works and charitable activities are also used frequently. Funny features are under-used, but certain to get placed. The manufacturer of a dog-grooming brush produced a tape about how proud pedigree owners got their pooches ready for Crufts: twenty-six out of thirty-five stations played it!
- *Have more than one interview on the tape to create a mini-feature.* One-to-one interviews are so predictable – more than one interview is livelier and generates greater audience interest.

About 3 weeks after mail-out, the production house

should organise a ring-round of the radio stations, to confirm placement and reply with a full breakdown of who played the tape and when. A satisfactory result would be around the 40 per cent success rate. Be wary of claims of 100 per cent – you may be dealing with an unscrupulous agency. Similarly, large stations such as Piccadilly Radio (Manchester) and LBC (London) don't use syndicated material, as a matter of broadcasting policy; if a syndicating agency purports to mail to such stations, you had better look elsewhere, for they will be likely to rip you off.

If time and care are taken to choose a reputable syndication house, and to create an innovative story-line, syndicated tapes are worth considering as placement aids. They are cheap to produce, and extra copies of the tapes can be made, for inclusion in press packs or as give-aways to clients or prospective clients.

Video news releases

Video news releases, or VNRs, are similar to syndicated radio tapes, but here the medium is television, not radio. With a VNR, short two- or three-minute interviews or pictures, with an accompanying script, are syndicated. The process was first engineered in the USA, where the hundreds of television and cable stations made the syndication of broadcast material a cost-effective and useful PR exercise.

In the UK only two companies to date produce such material: Newsflash, and Worldwide Television News, which is part of Independent Television News. Both the

BBC and ITV networks have used VNRs, and again success is determined at a play-rate of about 40 per cent. But the stations are cautious: using ready-to-view material could be looked upon as compromising their independence, and VNRs are only screened if the interest or novelty factor is high.

The first recorded instance of a VNR produced in the UK was in 1986, when American tourists boycotted Britain after the Libyan air bombing. A consortium of interested parties – including Trusthouse Forte, American Express, Avis and British Caledonian – clubbed together to produce a 90" VNR which was syndicated in America, showing the joys of holidaying in Britain. Play-rate was high – about 60 per cent – and, as associate producer on that VNR, I was particularly pleased that after the showing there was a marked increase in the number of US visitors to the UK. I'm not saying it was all due to the VNR, but I'm sure it helped.

Other notable VNR successes include highlights of the L'Oreal Trophy, showing the most colourful and weirdest hair fashions, which actually made the BBC Nine O'Clock News. Like syndicated tapes, VNRs can be carefully targeted to take in selected geographic areas, and, as mentioned above, can also be syndicated internationally. They are not cheap to produce – the average cost would be £7,000–£10,000 – but they are worth considering if broadcast placement is vitally important to a campaign.

Edited highlights of VNRs can be incorporated into existing corporate videos to give a longer shelf-life.

Surviving the Media Jungle

Cable and satellite television

There should be no mystique about dealing with cable and satellite television. Working with sky-based channels should be looked on as just another broadcast opportunity.

First in was cable. There are some forty cable operators currently broadcasting in the UK; some are the original cable networks which were installed more than 20 years ago, and which do not have the capacity to carry more than 4–6 channels. But in 1985 the Government set up the Cable Authority, which was awarded several 15-year franchises for the operation of 'wideband' cable systems (which can carry 25+ channels). Shorter licences have been granted to smaller SMATV (Satellite Master Antenna Television) systems, which provide cable services for entire offices, blocks of flats or hotels.

There are currently thirteen UK programme-makers who concentrate on cable programming. Cable subscribers can also tune in to the American CNN (Cable News Network) or to the pan-European SKY channel.

Cable lends itself easily to interactive television: subscribers could soon be swept into an age of home banking and home shopping, and play interactive games or make use of microcomputer software libraries – and all at the touch of a keypad. There are also possibilities for the provision of business services, such as data and facsimile transmission, and Mercury Telecommunications has installed test telephones in certain cable areas, whereby subscribers can obtain cheaper telephone calls.

In fact the opportunities offered by cable should be viewed more in terms of general consumer and business communications than in televisual terms. Cabling the nation is notoriously expensive – there is the inconvenience of digging up roads and neighbourhoods, and to date there are only about 283,816 households directly connected to cable in the UK, and just over 1 million households capable of receiving it.

The arrival of direct broadcasting by satellite (DBS) will probably have greater impact on the consumer's viewing habits. DBS beams television pictures directly to individual homes, via a receiving dish. No digging up roads, no mess, no fuss. For round about £200 the man in the street can buy a dish and set up his own pan-European viewing network, for subscribers can tune into French, German and Italian channels, as well as English-speaking programmes.

SKY Television was the first satellite programme provider to reach the British consumer when the Astra satellite was launched in 1988; currently it has the capacity to broadcast six channels, including the well-thought of SKY News, Eurosport, a non-stop sports channel, and the general entertainment SKY channel. SKY achieves a 51 per cent share of all television viewing in dish homes.

SKY will be strongly challenged by British Satellite Broadcasting (BSB), launched early in 1990, with five channels, including NOW, an information and lifestyle channel, The Movie Channel and the entertainment channel Galaxy.

Viewers will probably choose either BSB or SKY – they operate from different satellites and require different receiver dishes. To subscribe to both could prove very expensive. However, even though at the time of writing there are only some 600,000 subscribers to satellite TV, familiarity should breed not contempt but favourability.

Surviving the Media Jungle

As the system grows and develops, it will be interesting to see who wins the battle for the airwaves.

From an editorial placement point of view, there are two things to remember. Firstly, the new television should be viewed as an extension of your existing media relations strategy. Contact the individual stations to find out who produces the programmes you want your clients or your company's products to appear on. If they meet your specifications regarding audience profile, proceed just as you would with a terrestrial television outlet. The same ground rules apply. Secondly, bear in mind that until the new programmes are up and running – and this should take several years – cable and satellite are still open to suggestions. They will use excerpts of corporate videos within programmes, if these are relevant and shot to broadcast standard; they have been known to use VNRs; and they have introduced a new concept into broadcast terminology – the infomercial.

What is an infomercial?

At its simplest an infomercial is a slightly more commercialised VNR. If the VNR concentrates on strong storyline and news value, the infomercial has more of the gloss of an advertisement, with feature value. Screening at up to 5 minutes, infomercials have been around in the States for a long time: like advertisements, space is bought and screening time is paid for, but at a fraction of the cost of terrestrial rates.

In the UK infomercials have been pioneered on a test basis by Clyde Cablevision, but the process will no doubt become commonplace over the next few years, and negotiations with satellite programme suppliers a matter of course. The beauty of infomercials (rather like their print counterpart, advertorials) is that they are highly flexible: excerpts of corporate videos and VNRs can be edited together to create new programme ideas.

Infomercials can either be slotted in as natural breaks in existing advertising schedules, or viewed separately. On Clyde Cablevision, a separate network called The Consumer Channel was created, and the viewer was given a list of infomercials which he could key in to view at selected times. The best way to find out if a cable or satellite channel would be interested in an infomercial is to contact it direct. Promotional packages could certainly be created on an individual basis, which could lead to highly original programme placement.

One last word about satellite programming. It may not be useful to your media placement programmes yet, but it soon will be. Remember, you are not simply thinking *national*, you're thinking *European*. The single market means crossed boundaries and media overlaps. If your markets are out there, or could be out there, satellite television should not be ignored. On the contrary, it should be studied closely, to see how it fits into media strategy for 1992 and beyond.

Videotext

Videotext incorporates data and graphics viewed from a TV set. There are two forms: *Viewdata*, transmitted over phone lines (e.g. British Telecom's Prestel), and *Teletext*, transmitted via terrestrial networks (e.g. BBC's Ceefax and ITV's Oracle). Both are interactive systems, with the emphasis being on the business user for Prestel, the domestic user for Ceefax and Oracle.

Both show pages of information, accessed via a keypad. It is here that placement becomes a distinct possibility: features and news items can be sent to the relevant news desks, and offer yet another outlet for publicity. But do your research and target well. Teletext journalists work in the same time-honoured way, with individual section editors. The 'frames' or pages of data are simply part of an electronic newspaper.

From the PR viewpoint Oracle in particular is worth pursuing, as it is part of the independent television network. With access to 5.3 million viewers daily, it is open to PR suggestions: there have been many examples of organised competitions, special offers and other promotions, as well as direct editorial coverage.

If you are a small company, with a small PR budget and few staff, you may look at this chapter and think: 'This is for the big boys – VNRs and media tours don't apply to me'. But the point about this section of the book is that it talks about the future. I'm highlighting areas of promotion and publicity which will develop over the next few years, until they become as natural as sending out a press release. It's as well to know that they exist now. That way you'll never be caught out.

10

Whingeing and whining

When things don't work out in business, most executives take it on the chin. If a deal is lost, or a contract not renewed, you'll sigh, swear, but accept this as a normal part of corporate life. Yet if the media gets it wrong, the business world is up in arms. Before you know it, there's talk of legal action, long letters of protest, abusive phone calls to editors. Hold on. Law courts are notoriously slow and notoriously expensive. Few businessmen have either the time or the resources of such people as Sir James Goldsmith, who actively enjoys the pursuit of hounding the press, treating it rather like a blood-sport. Don't panic. Before you do anything, ask yourself whether the protest is really worth the aggravation.

How damaging is the error in the first place? If it's due to a misunderstanding or misreading of a press release, and its nature is not fundamentally harmful to your product or company, then telephone the editor or journalist concerned, and state your case. Don't come on too strong: attacking the media is never a good idea and you want to make sure you keep your friends in the press for other stories later on.

Be pleasant but firm, and try and get a simple retraction or clarification in the next edition of the newspaper or programme. Follow up the call with a letter, restating

Surviving the Media Jungle

the object of your conversation. The luxury goods company Alfred Dunhill Ltd does not like to be confused with Dunhill, the cigarette manufacturers. When a magazine mixed the names of the companies up, a swift telephone call and a friendly chat to the news desk made sure the mistake was duly noted in the following week's edition.

Most journalists will play ball if you treat them right, but some are intractable, and there will of course be times when it's best to turn a blind eye. Like Brer Fox – lie low.

In the long run, it's worth it. Good media relations are often a matter of give and take. Even though you may think that you give and the press takes, it does even out and work both ways. While you gnash your teeth in silent protest at the wilfulness of press, at least you can be comforted by the thought that:

(a) You and your company are probably much more sensitive to and aware of the issue than any reader or member of the public.
(b) News is soon over and done with – the editorial transgression will simply be yesterday's story before you know it, forgotten and buried deep in the archives.

But what if the press really goes too far? There are several options available to you. If you have been libelled, and your reputation lies in tatters, then you can bring an action in court. Newspapers and broadcast organisations over the last few years have reeled with the cost of paying out substantial damages to aggrieved members of the public, even though the cases we hear about tend to be confined to such well-known names as Derek Jameson, Koo Stark, or anything to do with *Private Eye*.

But to succeed in an action for libel, the plaintiff must prove without any reasonable doubt that the news source 'printed lies deliberately and maliciously in order to lower the plaintiff's standing in the minds of right-thinking people' (and that's a quote straight from the Defamation Act). This is an extremely difficult thing to prove, so be absolutely sure of your case before you begin legal action. Even then, the courts often err in favour of freedom of information and the press.

If you don't want to bring legal action, but simply want to rap the offending journalists and editors over the knuckles, you could take your complaint to the Press Council.

This august body was set up in 1953, and concerns itself solely with the newspaper industry. It was established 'to maintain the character of the British press in accordance with the highest professional and commercial standards', and 'to consider complaints about the conduct of the press, or the conduct of persons and organisations towards the press'.

If, after complaining directly to an editor, you still do not reach an equitable resolution, you should address your complaint in writing to the director of the Press Council (at the time of writing, Kenneth Morgan, OBE). The complaint will be investigated, and if the Council finds in your favour, the normal procedure is for the adjudication to be sent to the newspaper for publication.

There is also a 'fast track' procedure for factual inaccuracies in newspapers: after an individual has complained to the Council, an editor must publish a correction, or reply to the complainant within 3 working days. If he does not, he must submit to the Press Council's panel, and will probably be directed to retract the misleading information.

It must be said that the Press Council is concerned with ethics, not law. Its decisions are not legally binding upon newspapers, and you should remember that no one is allowed to seek legal action after contacting the Council – it is an either/or affair.

Even though the Press Council may be considered something of a toothless dragon, its reputation and directives are influential, and carry weight in opinion-forming circles. For this reason a complaint through the Council should be considered if you want to make a point, and hit home.

At the time of writing, the controversial Protection of Privacy Bill is making its passage through both Houses of Parliament, and, if implemented, should take effect in the early 1990s. The Bill is specifically designed to curb the powers of the press (both print and broadcast) when it comes to unreasonable and unbearable infringements of personal privacy. One thinks here of personal letters published without due consent in some tabloids and Sunday newspapers, or of the photographs that showed the Hillsborough victims being crushed to death against the barriers at the Leppings Lane end, which appeared in the *Sun*.

If a case were to come to court, the balance of the court would be tilted towards freedom of information, certainly, and a plaintiff would have to prove that it was in the public interest to withhold specific information. But this is the first time that an Act of Parliament has ordered either damages to be paid, or an injunction against publication to be granted, for infringement of privacy alone.

WHINGEING AND WHINING

As such, it is a historic piece of legislation, and one that will be scrutinised and worried over by the media for some time to come.

If your complaint relates to the broadcasting industry, there are also other paths you can pursue.

Obviously if it's a question of an interview, your first line of defence is to take control in the first place, making sure your comments are heard and understood. But if you have been misrepresented, the second, as with print, is to ask for a retraction or explanation, and it is by far the most preferable, and simplest way of correcting errors. Contact the producer or series producer as soon as possible, by telephone and then in writing, and try and have a tape-recorded or videotaped edition of the offending programme to back you up.

Bear in mind that both independent television and radio, and the BBC have similar guidelines when it comes to broadcast programming. They include:

- Informing interviewees of the format, subject matter and purpose of the programme, and the way their contribution will be used.

- Ensuring that edited highlights or extracts of programmes do not misrepresent an interviewee's viewpoint. Nor should separately recorded interviews be edited in such a way that it looks or sounds as if participants are conversing with each other. Severe disciplinary action is meted out to programmers who do not obey these guidelines.

If, despite this, you feel you have been misrepresented in any way, and a polite complaint gets no results, contact the Controller or Director of Programmes of the individual television or radio station, and when dealing with the BBC, enclose a copy for the Director-General as well, if your complaint is of a particularly serious nature.

Currently, broadcasting is undergoing great changes, and no more so than in independent television and radio. The government is planning a complete overhaul of their structure.

Hitherto ITV and independent radio have been governed by the IBA – the Independent Broadcasting Authority. The IBA was a statutory body set up to regulate the independent broadcasting organisations (both radio and television) and Channel 4, with wide-ranging powers, including that of hearing first-instance complaints. But the Broadcasting Bill, due to take effect in the early 1990s, proposes the abolition of the IBA and the Cable Authority, replacing these with the new Independent Television Commission (ITC) and a separate Radio Authority.

Whether the ITC and the new Radio Authority will have the same powers to deal with the complaints of the public as the old IBA is not yet clear. What is clear is that some redress can still be obtained at the hands of the Broadcasting Complaints Commission (BCC), which was set up to consider complaints of 'unjust or unfair treatment' or 'unwarranted infringement of privacy' in both BBC and ITV programmes.

Evidence must be submitted in writing before the BCC decides or not to proceed. Like many such government offices, the BCC is not noted for speed, and the process takes a long time. Even if it finds in favour of the plaintiff, the BCC cannot force a broadcasting body to apologise or broadcast the fact that it was in the wrong. What happens is that the Commission directs the offending organisation to publish a summary of the complaint and the BCC's findings in the *Radio Times* or *TV Times* and to screen it on the offending programme – which amounts to an apology of sorts.

Again the future of the BCC is in some doubt. The Broadcasting Bill recommends that it be merged, in the fullness of time, with the Broadcasting Standards Council, which was set up in 1988 and given statutory authority to reinforce standards relating to the screening of violence and sex. Whether this newly-formed body will be given the same powers as the BCC is again a subject for debate at the time of writing, although indications seem to show that it will.

Naturally this is not your only course of action. As stated, last resorts include action for libel, and possible redress under the forthcoming Protection of Privacy Act. But you may well be forgiven for thinking redress is all rather unsatisfactory, and that the dice are loaded in favour of the media.

Is it all worth the hassle? Probably not. If this chapter shows anything, it's that getting the media to admit they are wrong is both hazardous and fraught. Revenge may taste sweet, but not if it gives you blood pressure. Swallow your pride if you can. Unless you feel duty- and honour-bound to pursue an action against the press, do so at your peril.

It's even better if you can turn a potentially nasty situation to your advantage. One of the cleverest tricks I know was that organised by a big PR company, which was phoned by a frantic client. The client was a credit card company, and therein lay the problem: a hack on one of the tabloids, for a bit of a lark, had written off for

Surviving the Media Jungle

one such credit card in the name of his dog, and got one! 'It's the easiest thing in the world to cheat the card companies', ran the headlines. 'Even Bonzo will get credit!' The client was furious, threatening legal action, demanding a retraction, worrying about the firm's reputation.

'But you were in the wrong', said the wily account-handler. 'Make a joke of it. Admit you have slipped up. Say it doesn't happen often. Say you'll ensure that future applicants will be properly vetted. And apologise to the pooch: deliver a gold-plated doggie bowl and collar in a limousine, making sure you get all of Fleet Street's photographers there. You might as well get some good press out of this, and you'll get it if you show a sense of humour.'

It worked a treat.

11

Some sort of an ending

This is the point where, traditionally, the author writes a pithy epilogue – but I think that would be a rather grand finale for a light-hearted textbook. Instead I would simply like to summarise the chapters so far, and create a quick and breezy reference list for the busy executive.

Remember this list, and you're halfway to creating the kind of successful media relations you want for your company:

1 **Be aware**. Being aware means understanding your media markets. Get to know your trade publications and local media outlets well. Know their requirements, their deadlines, their schedules. Get to feel comfortable with the differences in style and tone of the national media, and exploit them to your advantage too.

2 **Be proactive, not just reactive**. By knowing what journalists want, you can anticipate their needs by giving them the appropriate stories. By reading widely, and knowing what is happening, not just in the trade, but in the business community and the world beyond, you can link your product to topical news items and hot stories, creating a news-

Surviving the Media Jungle

worthiness that wasn't there before, going beyond the press release.

3 **Keep the channels of communication flowing**. Phone up the press if you want to check data, or confirm whether a story is right for a particular media outlet. Tip them off if you get to hear of something you think they ought to know. Thank the press if they have covered a story well. A little neighbourhood watching never harmed anyone.

4 **Never badger**. Flogging a dead story is never a good idea, and obviously recycling old stories and pix is anathema. Neither does the press wish to be harassed by needless phone calls about boring product launches or press conferences. Learn to accept no for an answer – next time it will be yes. Be tactful – it will work wonders.

5 **Never attack the media**. Unless you really have to, you will nearly always come off worse if you take on the media. Keep your sense of humour.

6 **Never lie**. Lies will always be found out, and can create havoc for you and your company – not the kind of headlines you've been working for. Honesty is aways the best policy in media relations. If you don't know something, say so – and add you will find out as soon as you can. Never speculate – you might find yourself in hot water.

7 **Be accessible**. Take journalists' calls. Don't be over-defensive or act as if you had something to hide. Never say 'No comment'. Be open with journalists. You don't have to have a press office *per se*, but give

SOME SORT OF AN ENDING

them a contact name and number, and make sure there is always someone available at that number. This also applies to after-hours and weekends; every company should have a press contact available 24 hours of the day.

8 **Organise your information sources**. Press releases, background notes, publicity photographs, cuttings, media contact lists should always be to hand, updated and available to you, the press and any other source of inquiry.

9 **Create media goals**. There is a subtle difference between expecting too much of a media relations campaign, which is usually fatal and ends in disappointment, and setting definitely attainable, and regularly reviewed and updated, goals for coverage. Make a list of the print, broadcast, trade, local and national media coverage your company really needs, and go for it. Goals give you the incentive to pursue campaigns, and the challenge creates its own rewards.

10 **Never forget: once a journalist, always a journalist**. Treat journalists as fellow professionals, respect them, show you understand the way they operate and work with them to create the stories you both need. But never take the press for granted: even if a journo becomes your friend, his duty remains first and foremost to the media outlet he represents. That means no 'off the record' tit-bits, no trade-offs, no presumptions. Similarly you will never get a headline by chatting a journalist up when there's no story to back it up, whether you advertise in the

Surviving the Media Jungle

publication or not. As someone once said, there's no such thing as a free lunch, and most hacks know it.

Good luck!

Appendix I Getting started

Sources of media information

ADVANCE: two-monthly reference guide to forthcoming editorial features, 2 Prebendal Court, Oxford Road, Aylesbury, Bucks, HP19 3EY.

Benn's Media Directory: published in two volumes, UK and International, provides media data of 197 countries, including cable and satellite outlets. Benn Business Information Services Ltd, PO Box 20, Sovereign Way, Tonbridge, Kent TN9 1RQ. Tel: 0732 32666.

The Blue Book of British Broadcasting: published annually by monitoring service Tellex Monitors, a comprehensive handbook for professionals on UK broadcasting outlets. Tellex Monitors Ltd, 47 Gray's Inn Road, London WC1X 8PR.

British Rate & Data (BRAD): good source of media information, including national and regional newspapers, TV and radio, updated monthly. Maclean Hunter House, Chalk Lane, Cockfosters Road, Barnet, Herts EN4 0BU. Tel: 01 441 6644.

Editors: published in six volumes, *Editors* includes newspaper, magazine and broadcast outlets, plus readership profile and forthcoming special features. Published quarterly. PR Newslink, 9–10 Great Sutton Street, London EC1V 0BX. Tel: 01 251 9000.

Surviving the Media Jungle

Hollis Press & Public Relations Annual: listing all major UK and many international PR consultancies, creative service agencies, blue-chip company PROs, etc. Invaluable. Contact House, Lower Hampton Road, Sunbury-on-Thames, MDX TW16 5HG.

PIMS Media Directory: a monthly directory listing all UK media. A separate European edition is also available. PIMS London plc, PIMS House, 4 St John's Place, London EC1M 4AH. Tel: 01 250 0870.

PNA Media Link: comprehensive two-monthly guide to UK media. PNA, 13–19 Curtain Road, London EC2A 3LT. Tel: 01 377 2521.

PR Planner (Europe and UK): comprehensive guide to media contacts. Media Information Ltd, Hale House, 290–6 Green Lanes, London N13 5TP.

Willings Press Guide: Windsor Court, East Grinstead House, East Grinstead, W. Sussex RH19 IXA. Tel: 0342 26972.

Magazines

Broadcast: the broadcast industry bible, 100 Avenue Road, Swiss Cottage, London NW3. Tel: 01 935 6611.

Campaign: the advertising industry bible, but worth consulting, 22 Lancaster Gate, London W2. Tel: 01 402 4200.

Media Week: an excellent industry overview, 20–2 Wellington Street, London WC2E 7DD. Tel: 01 379 5155.

PR Week: the PR industry bible, 22 Lancaster Gate, London W2. Tel: 01 402 4200.

APPENDIX I   GETTING STARTED

UK Press Gazette: the hack's bible. Bouverie Publishing, 244-9 Temple Chambers, Temple Avenue, London EC4.

Press-cutting agencies

Durrants Press Cutting Bureau: 103 Whitecross Street, London EC1Y 8QT. Tel: 588 3671.

Newsclip (UK) Ltd: 52-3 Fetter Lane, London EC4. Tel: 01 353 7191.

Romeike and Curtice Ltd: Hale House, 290-6 Green Lanes, London N13 5TP. Tel: 01 882 0155.

Organisations

Institute of Journalists: the second professional body for journalists, broadcasters, PROs. Suite 2, Dock Offices, Surrey Quays, Lower Road, Docklands, London SE16 2YS. Tel: 01 252 1187.

Institute of Public Relations: The Old Trading House, 15 Northburgh Street, London EC1V 0PR. Tel: 01 253 5151.

National Union of Journalists: official trade union for journalists, public relations officers, etc. Acorn House, 314 Gray's Inn Road, London WC1X 8DP. Tel: 01 278 7916.

Public Relations Consultants Association: the trade association for public relations consultancies. Premier House, 10 Greycoat Place, London SW1P 1SB. Tel: 01 222 8866.

Photography

British Institute of Professional Photography: 2 Amwell End, Ware, Herts. SG12 9HN. Tel: 0920 4011.

Royal Photographic Society: The Octagon, Milson Street, Bath BA1 1DN. Tel: 0225 62841.

Video news releases

Newsflash: 40 Floral Street, London W1. Tel: 01 379 0565.

Worldwide Television News, 33–6 Foley Street, London W1. Tel: 01 323 3255.

Television training and media training

Burson-Marsteller Ltd: 24–8 Bloomsbury Way, London WC1. Tel: 01 831 6262.

CTVC: Hillside Studios, Merry Hill Road, Bushey, Watford WD2 1DR. Tel: 01 950 4426.

Wadlow Grosvenor Ltd: 19 Grosvenor Street, London W1. Tel: 409 1225.

Media Interviews Ltd: 87 Charlotte Street, London W1. Tel: 01 631 5424.

Public relations training courses

Ashridge College of Further Education: Berkhamsted, Herts HP4 1NS. Tel: 044284 3491/2311.

APPENDIX I   GETTING STARTED

Cranfield School of Management: Cranfield, Bedford MK43 0AL. Tel: 0234 751122.

Institute of Marketing: Moor Hall, Cookham, Maidenhead, Berks SL6 9QH. Tel: 06285 24922.

Interact International Seminars Ltd: 10a High Street, Tunbridge Wells, Kent TN1A 1AA. Tel: 0892 515222.

London Business School: Sussex Place, Regent's Park, London NW1 4SA. Tel: 01 262 5050.

London Chamber of Commerce and Industry (LCCI): Examinations Board, Marlow House, Station Road, Sidcup, Kent DA15 7BJ. Tel: 01 302 0261.

University of Bradford: Management Centre, Emm Lane, Bradford, W. Yorkshire BD9 4JL. Tel: 0274 42299.

University of Stirling: Stirling, Scotland FK8 4LF. Tel: 0786 73171.

Watford College: Hempstead Road, Watford, Herts WD1 3EZ. Tel: 0923 57500.

Broadcast media contacts
(National newspapers will be found in any media directory.)

BBC: Headquarters, Broadcasting House, Portland Place, London W1A 1AA. Tel: 01 580 4468.

British Satellite Broadcasting: The Marco Polo Building, Queenstown Road, London SW8.

Surviving the Media Jungle

Broadcasting Complaints Commission: Grosvenor Gardens House, 35–7 Grosvenor Gardens, London SW1W 0BS. Tel: 01 630 1966.

Cable Authority: Gillingham House, 38–44 Gillingham Street, London SW1V 1HU. Tel: 01 821 6161.

Ceefax: BBC Television Centre, Wood Lane, London W12 7RJ. Tel: 01 743 8000.

IBA: Headquarters, 70 Brompton Road, London SW3 1EY. Tel: 01 584 7011. NB: IBA to be abolished.

Independent Television Association Ltd: 56 Mortimer Street, London W1N 8AN. Tel: 01 636 6866. NB: Independent Television undergoing radical changes.

Oracle: Craven House, 25–32 Marshall Street, London W1V 1LL. Tel: 01 434 3121.

Press Council: Salisbury Square, London EC4. Tel: 01 353 1248.

SKY Television: 6 Centaur's Business Park, Grant Way, off Syon Lane, Isleworth, Middlesex TW7 5QD. Tel: 01 782 3000.

Super Channel: Europe's leading international TV service from cable. Vision House, 19–22 Rathbone Place, London W1P 1DF. Tel: 01 631 5050.

WH Smith Television: The Quadrangle, 180 Wardour Street, London W1V 4AE. Tel: 01 439 1177.

Bibliography

Bland, Michael (1987) *Be Your Own PR Man* (Kogan Page).
Broadcasting in the 90s: Competition, Choice and Quality (HMSO).
Hart, N. and Lamb. G. (1981)   *A Career in Marketing, Advertising and Public Relations* (Heinemann).
Haywood, Roger (1984) *All About PR* (The McGraw-Hill Marketing Series).
Jefkins, Frank (1986)   *Planned Press and Public Relations* (Blackie).
Lewis, Mel (1987) *Writing to Win* (McGraw-Hill).
Morley, D. and Whitaker, B. (1983)   *The Press, Radio and Television: an introduction to the media* (Comedia).
Plain Words (HMSO).
PR Marketing and Public Relations Handbook (Kogan Page).
Quiller-Couch, Sir Arthur   *On the Art of Writing*.
Waterhouse, Keith (1989) *Waterhouse on Newspaper Style* (Viking)

Index

1992, 78, 187
40 Minutes (BBC TV), 148

Adams, Kim, 45
agencies, picture, *see* picture agencies
agencies, press cuttings, *see* press cuttings agencies
AIDS, 73
Alexander Technique, 167
American Express, 183
Amstrad, 130
Andrex, 71
'Arthur' the white cat, 71
Aspects of Love, 128
ASTRA satellite, 65, 185
Australia (Bi-centenary), 65
Avis, 183

BAT (British American Tobacco) 169
BBC
    Controller of Programmes, 193–4
    Director-General, 194
BBC Radio 4, 27, 31–6, 37
BBC World Service, 37
Beatles, The, 78

Bejam, 152
Bellamy, David, 63–4
Bergerac, 135
Bernstein, David, 94
Beta-Blockers, 167
BIG DEAL (test), 47–8, 147
Bland, Michael, 62
Body Shop, The, 74
Bordes, Pamella, 59–60
Brad (British Rate & Data), 13
Breakfast Time (BBC TV), 34, 37
British Caledonian Airways, 183
British Heart Foundation, 68, 77
British Telecom, 65, 106, 187
Broadcast, 53
Broadcast News, 37
Broadcasting Bill, The, 155, 194
Broadcasting Complaints Commission (BCC), 194–5
Broadcasting House, 156
Broadcasting Standards Council, 195

Surviving the Media Jungle

BSB (British Satellite Broadcasting), 185–6
Burchill, Julie, 24
Burson-Marsteller, 53, 172
Business Programme, The, 23
BVU, 151–2

Cable Authority, The, 184, 194
cable television, 184–7
Cameron, James, 54
captions (in photography), 111–12
Cash and Carry Wholesaler, 51
catering, 122, 124–5, 126, 127, 136
Ceefax, 187–8
Channel Four, 37, 39, 194
Christie's (auctioneers), 40, 41–2, 78–9
Churchill, Jill, 46
Cinzano (commercial), 76
Clouds, 117–18
Clyde Cablevision, 186–7
CNN (Cable News Network), 184
Collins, Joan, 76
Communiqué, 87–8
'Community Chest' (campaign), 63–4, 74
complaints, 189–96
Concorde, 72
Conference & Exhibitions Monthly, 75
Conservation Foundation, The, 63

Consumer Channel, The, 187
copyright, 112
Creative Business, The, 94
Crematorium Monthly, 51
Crocodile Dundee, 65

Daily Express, 16, 27, 48, 54, 131
Daily Mail, 16, 17, 20–21, 27–31, 48, 62
Daily Mirror, 16, 17, 22–3, 130
Daily Telegraph, 16, 17, 47, 128, 136
Dance with a Stranger, 78
Day, Sir Robin, 24, 171
DBS (Direct Broadcasting by Satellite), 65, 185–6
Defamation Act, the, 191
'Delight!' (margarine), 66
directories, 13, 51, 75, 105, 130
DIY Monthly, 49
Dulux Dog, the, 71
Dunhill, Alfred, Ltd., 190

Editors, 13, 105, 130
Electrical and Retail Trader, 49
El Vino's, 29, 67
embargoes, 92
Eurosport (Channel), 185
Eurovision (satellite link), 39
Evening Standard, 55
Exhibitions Bulletin, 128

FA (Football Association), 161

INDEX

facility visits, 120–23
Family Circle, 46, 55
Farley Health Products, 177–9
faxes, 99
Financial Times, 16, 50, 95, 128, 136
format (photographic), 109–10
Frayn, Michael, 117–18
Friends of the Earth, 74

Galaxy (Channel), 185
Gardeners' World, 49
Gillette, 74
Goldsmith, Sir James, 189
Guardian, The, 16
Guinness (take-over affair), 24–5

Hall, Mervyn, 3, 37, 39–42
Hampshire, Susan, 63–4, 78
Harding, Phil, 31–6, 132
High and Mighty (clothes shop), 108
Hillsborough (football tragedy), 31–3, 161, 192
Hennessy, Bill (Associates), 105
Holiday, 148
Hollis, 105
Honeycombe, Gordon, 48
Hotel and Catering Monthly, 51
House and Garden, 49
Hulton Picture Library, 112

IBA (Independent Broadcasting Authority), 194
Independent Radio News (IRN), 156
Independent, The, 16, 25
Independent on Sunday, The, 16
infomercials, 186–7
Institute of Professional Photography, 105
interviews (how to handle), 153–75
IPC, 128
ITC (Independent Television Commission), 194
ITN, 36–41, 71, 78, 157, 182–3

James, Clive, 48
Jameson, Derek, 191
jargon, 94, 165–6
Jersey, States of, 135–6

Kennedy, Philippa, 46
Kinnock, Neil, 165

LBC, 23, 37, 156, 182
Legal and General (Insurance Co.), 62
Leichner (make-up), 165
Lennon, John, 40, 41
Lepidopterist, The, 52
libel, 190–96
live-links, 153
local radio, 155
London Newspaper Group, 45

Surviving the Media Jungle

L'Oreal (Trophy, the), 183
Lusardi, Linda, 77

Mail on Sunday, 16
Manchester Evening News, 55
Marks & Spencer, 153
MARPLAN (poll), 61
'Marvel', 68, 77
Mastermind, 159
Matsushita Corporation, 53, 135
McGregor, Sue, 150
media tours, 177–80
Metal Box, 74
Miller, Jonathan, 165
Mirman, Sophie, 72
'Miss Pears', 70
Money Programme, The, 23
Morgan, Kenneth, O.B.E., 191
MORI (poll), 61
Mortality and Morbidity Weekly, 51
Movie Channel, the, 185

National Dairy Council, 63
National Magazine House, 128
National Union of Journalists (NUJ), 105, 112
Natural History, British Museum of, 113
Natural World, The, 149
nerves, 167
Nettles, John, 135
News at 5.40 (ITN), 38–40, 41

News at One (ITN), 38–40
News At Ten, 25, 37–42
news angles, 59–79
Newsflash (company), 182
News of the World, 16
New York Times, 43
Nine O'Clock News (BBC), 183
Nolan, Dee, 44–5, 52
Nott, John, 171
NOW (Satellite Channel), 185

Observer, The, 16
Open University, the, 72
opinion polls (see surveys)
Oracle (ITV), 187–8
Orpington News Shopper, 103, 110
Out of Africa, 78

Panorama (BBC TV), 149, 169
phone-ins, 153
photo-calls, 123–5
photography (for PR), 101–14
photo libraries, 112–14
Piccadilly Radio, 182
Pick of the Week (BBC Radio), 33
picture agencies, 112–14
PIMS, 51
Planet Earth (picture library), 112
PM (BBC Radio), 35
PNA, 13, 51, 105, 130
Premier Brands, 68
Press Association, The, 43

INDEX

press briefings, 119–20
press conferences, 125–143
Press Council, The, 191–2
press cuttings agencies, 15
press-kit, 137–9
press releases, 81–99
Prestel, 187–8
Privacy, Protection of (Bill), 192, 195
Private Eye, 191
PR Newslink, 13
Profumo (affair), 24
PR Week, 44, 128

Q + A sessions, 134

Radio Authority, The, 194
Radio Times, 17, 195
Reader's Digest, 140–41
Reagan, Ronald, 174
Redferns (Picture Library), 112
Redhead, Brian, 24, 32, 33, 150
Red Rose Radio, 23
Reuters, 43
Revolution, French, 65
Roddick, Anita, 74
Roe, Erica, 71–2
Rook, Jean, 24
Rossiter, Leonard, 76
Rudge, Gerald, 27–31

Saint Tiggywinkles (Animal Hospital), 63–4
satellite channels, 37, 184–7
Scandal, 78
Silhouette (publishers), 62

Sky Channel, 37, 184–6
'Slim and Save Lives' (campaign), 68
SMATV (Satellite Master Antenna Television), 184
Sock Shop, The, 72
Sotheby's (auctioneers), 42, 78
South Bank Show, The (ITV), 148
Spillers, 71
Squarial (satellite dish), 53, 135
Star, The, 16, 72, 130
Stark, Koo, 191
Sunday Correspondent, 16
Sunday Express, 16
Sunday People, 16
Sunday Sport, 16
Sunday Telegraph, 16
Sunday Times, 16, 120
Sun, The, 16, 59–60
surveys, 61–2
syndicated radio tapes, 180–82

targeting, 43–57
Teletext, 187–8
Televisual, 53–4
Terrys, 75
Thames News, 76
Thatcher, Margaret, 163, 165
That's Life! (BBC TV), 73
This Week (ITV), 148, 168
Times, The, 16, 17–20, 48, 60, 61, 75

Today (newspaper), 16
Today Programme, The (BBC Radio), 27, 31–6, 132, 148
Tomorrow's World, 148
training (media), 161
Trusthouse Forte, 63–4, 74, 183
TV-am, 37
TV Times, 14, 195

UK Press Gazette, 75
Undertakers Gazette, 51
UNS, 43

Veuve Clicquot (Businesswoman of the Year Award), 72
videotext, 187–8
Viewdata, 187–8

VNR (video news release), 182–3, 186–7

Watchdog (ITV), 161
Willings, 13, 51
Winalot, 71
wire services, 43
Woman's Hour (BBC Radio), 148, 152–3
Woman's Own, 13
Woman's Realm, 13
World Tonight, The, 156
Writers' & Artists' Yearbook, 75
WTN (Worldwide Television News), 39, 182–3

You and Your Barclaycard, 49

Zerb, 52